Journal of the Shenandoah Valley During the Civil War Era

Volume IV
2021

Jonathan A. Noyalas
Editor

A publication of Shenandoah University's McCormick Civil War Institute

ISSN: 2639-6815
ISBN: 979-8633360950

Manuscript Submissions and Books for Review

The *Journal of the Shenandoah Valley During the Civil War* is published annually by Shenandoah University's McCormick Civil War Institute. Manuscript submissions can be sent to the editor at jnoyalas01@su.edu. Manuscripts should not exceed 10,000 words in length (including footnotes). Books for review consideration can be sent to the editor at the *Journal of the Shenandoah Valley During the Civil War's* editorial home: Jonathan A. Noyalas, director McCormick Civil War Institute, Davis Hall 115, 1460 University Drive, Winchester, VA 22601.

Cover image, "Entrance to Camp Russell, 1885" photographed by Warren, Waltham, published by Black & Co., Boston, 1885, courtesy of Jonathan A. Noyalas, private collection.

Any opinions expressed in this publication are solely those of the contributing author and do not necessarily reflect the viewpoints of the editor, editorial advisory board, Shenandoah University, or the McCormick Civil War Institute.

Contents

From the Editor

Feature Essays

Book Reviews

From the Editor

Reflecting on Catton's *America Goes to War*

Jonathan A. Noyalas

In the spring of 1958 historian Bruce Catton journeyed to Wesleyan University in Middletown, Connecticut, to deliver a series of seven lectures focusing on everything from the Civil War as the first modern war, Ulysses S. Grant's presidency, and the unfinished task remaining before the citizens of the United States on the eve of the Civil War's centennial to fulfil the promise of emancipation. Wesleyan University found Catton's remarks so poignant that they published his lectures in *America Goes to War*. Although a rather slim volume, one could make the argument that Catton's musings in those 126 pages are arguably the most significant thoughts he ever committed to paper as the book is not merely a recounting of various moments in the Civil War era's history, but provides perspective on how individuals should view that history.

To some individuals at the time Catton spoke at Wesleyan, and to some today, the Civil War was a simpler, romantic period. Viewing Civil War era history in this light frustrated Catton. In the introduction to *America Goes to War* Catton wrote that the Civil War "is becoming to us, what it never was to the people who had taken part in it, something romantic, a bright and colorful splash in the center of the slightly drab story of this country's nineteenth-century development."[1] Catton believed viewing the Civil War era in this light problematic. "The only real trouble in romanticizing the Civil

---

[1] Bruce Catton, *America Goes to War* (Middletown, CT: Wesleyan University Press, 1958), 11.

War in this way—in looking on it as, essentially, something that we contrived in the high and far-off times for our own amusement—we are missing the point of it. And the real point is a matter that we can very profitably meditate on for a time, because it still has a time for us."[2]

Catton's observation is as poignant today as it was in 1958. This volume is inspired in part by Catton's musings in Connecticut more than six decades ago. The roster of Cool Spring's Confederate dead, the entries from Ephraim Burket's diary, the sacrifices of Rhode Islanders in the 1864 Shenandoah Campaign, and excerpts from the Southern Claims Commission that appear in this volume provide clear evidence that holding romantic notions about the Civil War era is folly. There is little romance in young men being killed in combat, nothing glorious about war transforming wives into widows or making children fatherless.

Beyond the contributions to this volume which shuck some of the romanticism away from the Shenandoah Valley's Civil War era story, this volume contains a slate of book reviews highlighting books directly related to the Shenandoah Valley's Civil War era story or ones that can in some way provide historical context and offer a framework for better understanding various aspects of the Valley's Civil War era history.

---

[2] Catton, *America Goes to War*, 12.

"Life was Extinct"
A Roster of Cool Spring's Confederate Dead

Jake Gabriele, Victor Herrera, Brandy N. Noyalas,
Jonathan A. Noyalas, Kimberely Vanscoy Oliveto,
Nicole A. Roland, Shelby R. Shrader, and
Steven R. Stabler

Among the fifteen major battles fought in the Shenandoah Valley, the Battle of Cool Spring is arguably the least recognizable.[1] The battles of Confederate general Thomas J. "Stonewall" Jackson's 1862 Valley Campaign and Union general Philip H. Sheridan's 1864 Shenandoah Campaign are well-known and have received much attention from scholars. The Battle of New Market, statistically smaller than Cool Spring, has received wide-attention, its popularity stemming in part from the role cadets from the Virginia Military Institute played at the battle. Although not as familiar as Jackson's victory at Port Republic or Sheridan's smashing success at Cedar Creek, to the Union and Confederate soldiers who fought

---

[1] While 326 different military actions occurred in the Shenandoah Valley, the fifteen major battles considered here are: the First Battle of Kernstown (March 23, 1862); Battle of McDowell (May 8, 1862); Battle of Front Royal (May 23, 1862); First Battle of Winchester (May 25, 1862); Battle of Cross Keys (June 8, 1862); Battle of Port Republic (June 9, 1862); Second Battle of Winchester (June 13-15, 1863); Battle of New Market (May 15, 1864); Battle of Piedmont (June 5, 1864); Battle of Cool Spring (July 18, 1864); Second Battle of Kernstown (July 24, 1864); Third Battle of Winchester (September 19, 1864); Battle of Fisher's Hill (September 22, 1864); Battle of Tom's Brook (October 9, 1864); and the Battle of Cedar Creek (October 19, 1864). Heritage Partners, Inc. and John Milner Associates, Inc., *Shenandoah Valley Battlefields National Historic District: Final Management Plan* (New Market, VA: Shenandoah Valley Battlefields National Historic District, 2000), i. Some lists might include additional engagements such as Battle of Rutherford's Farm (July 20, 1864) and Battle of Waynesboro (March 2, 1865).

and sacrificed at Cool Spring and to the families of those who had husbands, sons, and brothers killed in the battle, the fighting along the banks of the Shenandoah on July 18, 1864, proved the war's most significant moment.

Since Shenandoah University acquired 195 acres of the Cool Spring Battlefield in 2013, Shenandoah University's McCormick Civil War Institute assumed the awesome and important responsibility of all interpretive and educational efforts at Cool Spring. Amidst the time-consuming work of developing tours, designing exhibitions, conducting special programs, and installing interpretive signs, the McCormick Civil War Institute, since the summer of 2018, has been identifying and researching the backgrounds of the Union and Confederate soldiers killed at Cool Spring or those who died as a result of wounds received at the battle. This roster of Confederate dead is an important step in resurrecting individual stories from the Battle of Cool Spring which illuminates the battle's impact on soldiers, comrades, families, and communities. This roster completes the McCormick Civil War Institute's multi-year project on the battle's dead. A roster of Union soldiers killed at the Battle of Cool Spring appears in volume 3 of *Journal of the Shenandoah Valley During the Civil War Era*.

Among the sixty-four identifiable Confederate soldiers either killed or mortally wounded at the Battle of Cool Spring, the average age was twenty-seven, the same average age as Union troops who perished at the battle.[2] Five Confederate soldiers killed or mortally wounded at Cool Spring either enslaved or came from families who enslaved human beings. The youngest Confederate soldier killed at Cool Spring was William A. Shofner, an eighteen-year-old private in the 53rd North Carolina Infantry who mustered into service three months prior to battle. At forty-eight-years-old Corporal Louis Redmon Wells, a native of Tarboro, North Carolina, married with six children, who served in the 30th North Carolina, was the oldest Confederate soldier killed at Cool Spring. While records do not usually specify the type of fatal wounds suffered at the battle, some do. Of the ten soldiers for whom a clear fatal wound

---

[2] Jake Gabriele, Victor Herrera, Jonathan A. Noyalas, Sarah Powell & Shelby R. Shrader, "The Shenandoah Chanting its Endless Requiem," *Journal of the Shenandoah Valley During the Civil War Era* 3 (2020): 4.

is specified two suffered lethal chest wounds, one to his neck, one had an artery severed in his right leg, one shot in the head, two shot through the bowels, one suffered a mortal shoulder wound, and two were "mutilated" or "mangled" by artillery shells.

In addition to providing a demographic snapshot of these Confederate dead, this roster offers a powerful reminder of war's tragic consequences. What happens on a battlefield in any conflict, at any time, and in any place not only results in victory or defeat, captures, wounding, and deaths, but produces widows and orphans. At least eight of the Confederate soldiers who died were married and had children.

This roster then, serves not only as a tool to assist those who study the Battle of Cool Spring, but provides a lens through which individuals can contemplate the gruesome cost of war and what happens when a people become divided to an unbridgeable point.

2nd North Carolina Infantry

Adam Hartman (private)

A farmer from Davidson County, North Carolina, Adam Hartman enlisted in Company C, 2nd North Carolina Infantry on September 27, 1863. The forty-two-year-old farmer was married with four children.[3] During the Battle of Cool Spring, Hartman was shot in his back and right shoulder. He died at Mount Jackson, Virginia.[4]

Henry J. Jones (corporal)

Born on January 12, 1840, in Wilson County, North Carolina, Henry J. Jones was married with one young child and worked as a farm laborer when he enlisted in Company D, 43rd North Carolina Infantry on July 18, 1861.[5] He was promoted to corporal on April 10, 1863. He was admitted to Episcopal Church Hospital in Williamsburg, Virginia, on May 15, 1863, to be treated for a gunshot wound. It is unknown how he sustained this injury. He was cleared

---

[3] 1860 U.S. Census, Northern Division, Davidson, North Carolina, Adam Hartman, May 2, 2020, Ancestry.com.
[4] American Civil War Research Database, "Adam Hartman," Historical Data Systems, June 3, 2020, www.civilwardata.com.
[5] 1860 U.S. Census, Old Fields, Wilson, North Carolina, Henry Jones, April 28, 2020, Ancestry.com.

to return to active duty September 9, 1863. Jones was mortally wounded during the Battle of Cool Spring and died on July 22. He is buried in Stonewall Confederate Cemetery in Winchester, Virginia. His memorial marker indicates he served as "Acting Ensign and Color Bearer" during the battle.[6]

Walter Stallings (lieutenant colonel)

Twenty-seven-year-old Walter Stallings enlisted in the 2nd North Carolina Infantry on May 16, 1861. He joined the regiment at the rank of captain. Stallings was promoted to major in October 1862 and to lieutenant colonel on May 2, 1863. Records indicate that Stallings was wounded "early in the action" on May 3, 1863, at Chancellorsville. He was killed at the Battle of Cool Spring. Stallings is buried in the Stonewall Confederate Cemetery in Winchester, Virginia.[7]

Colonel Walter Stallings' tombstone in the Stonewall Confederate Cemetery
(*Photo by Jonathan A. Noyalas*)

---

[6] Henry J. Jones, 2nd North Carolina Infantry, Compiled Service Record (hereafter cited as CSR), National Archives and Records Administration, Washington, D.C. (hereafter cited as NARA).
[7] Walter Stallings, 2nd North Carolina Infantry, CSR, NARA.

2nd North Carolina Infantry Battalion

William D. Craven (sergeant)

Nineteen-year-old William D. Craven enlisted in Company G, 2nd North Carolina Infantry on September 19, 1862. He mustered into service with the 2nd North Carolina on January 18, 1863. He was singled out for "act[s of] gallantry at Gettysburg." Craven was promoted to sergeant on April 15, 1864. He sustained a mortal wound to the chest during the Battle of Cool Spring. He died at the General Hospital in Winchester on July 26, 1864.[8] He is buried in Stonewall Confederate Cemetery.

Martin Meese (private)

Martin Meese enlisted in Company H, 2nd North Carolina Infantry Battalion on June 28, 1864, in Marshall (Madison County). He is believed to have been killed during the Battle of Cool Spring. An unknown North Carolina grave marked "M.M" at Stonewall Confederate Cemetery could mark the location of his remains. The date of death is listed as July 26, 1864.[9]

Aaron Pickard (sergeant)

Davidson resident Aaron Pickard enlisted in Company G, 2nd North Carolina Infantry Battalion in September 1861. The nineteen-year-old mustered into service on January 18, 1862. Muster rolls dated February 28 to October 31, 1862 indicate "Bounty and 6 months commutation money due and unpaid." Pickard was promoted to sergeant on January 15, 1863. He was hospitalized in mid-July and furloughed from August 1 to September 1 by Surgeon Thomas Hill. Pickard was at home on furlough again between January and February 1864. He was mortally wounded during the Battle of Cool Spring and died on July 19, 1864. The location of his remains is unknown.[10]

4th North Carolina Infantry

David S. Bustle (private)

---

8 William D. Craven, 2nd North Carolina Infantry Battalion, CSR, NARA.
9 Martin Meese, 2nd North Carolina Infantry Battalion, CSR, NARA.
10 Aaron Pickard, 2nd North Carolina Infantry Battalion, CSR, NARA.

David S. Bustle was twenty years old when he enlisted "for the war" in Company C, 4th North Carolina Infantry on June 7, 1861, in Statesville. He was present on all company muster rolls, but was marked "sick since Oct. 2, 1861" on the September-October muster roll. He was killed in action during the Battle of Cool Spring. He is buried in Stonewall Confederate Cemetery in Winchester.[11]

Arthur Evans (private)
A resident of Edgecombe, North Carolina, Arthur Evans was working as a miller when he enlisted in Company F, 4th North Carolina Infantry on April 18, 1862. He was married and had a young son, Glenn Junius.[12] In the spring of 1864, Evans was marked absent from his unit, on extra daily duty as fisherman. Company receipt rolls indicate he signed his name "by mark." Arthur Evans was killed in action during the Battle of Cool Spring.[13] He is buried in the Evans Family Cemetery in Wilson, North Carolina.[14]

Martin Snow (private)
Martin Snow enlisted in the 4th North Carolina Infantry on May 29, 1861. Reports indicate that he was captured near Fredericksburg on May 3, 1863. One week later he was exchanged and returned to his unit. During the Battle of Cool Spring, Snow served in the regiment's color guard and was killed during one of General Robert Rodes' assaults against Colonel Joseph Thoburn's northern flank.[15] After the conflict, John Alexander Stikeleather, the regiment's color-bearer, wrote of Snow's death: "When I come to think and speak of Martin Snow I feel that I am treading on sacred ground... And, to-day I cherish his memory with a chastened pleasure known only to myself... A few minutes before he fell, I call[ed] his attention to the confused [state] of the enemy in our immediate front, and remarked that one well directed shot, would do more than ordinary execution. He took in the situation at a glance, and with face elate[d]

---

[11] David S. Bustle, 4th North Carolina Infantry, CSR, NARA.
[12] 1860 U.S. Census, Edgecombe, North Carolina, Arthur Evans, April 26, 2020, Ancestry.com.
[13] Arthur Evans, 4th North Carolina Infantry, CSR, NARA
[14] National Cemetery Administration, U.S. Veterans' Gravesites, Arthur Evans, April 26, 2020, Ancestry.com.
[15] Martin Snow, 4th North Carolina Infantry, CSR, NARA.

leveled his gun and fired; before he could lower his gun, a ball from an enemies [*sic*] gun struck him in the neck just below the left ear, when he fell right at my side, and in ten seconds life was extinct."[16] The whereabouts of Snow's remains are unknown.

James Hall Wood (colonel)

Colonel James Hall Wood
(*Histories of the Several Regiments and Battalions from North Carolina*, 1901)

On May 16, 1861, twenty-year-old James Hall Wood of Rowan County, North Carolina, was commissioned as the captain of Company B, 4th North Carolina Infantry, nicknamed the "Scotch Ireland Grays."[17] After a year of leading his company in multiple engagements, Wood was promoted to major on July 2, 1862. This began his rapid rise through the ranks as he was promoted to lieutenant colonel in December of that year. Lieutenant Colonel Wood appears on battle reports from Gettysburg, as he helped lead the 4th North Carolina Infantry in attacks on Culps Hill. Wood was promoted to colonel on May 19, 1864, two months before he was killed at the Battle of Cool Spring.[18]

---

[16] Unpublished Reminiscences of John Alexander Stikeleather, 4th North Carolina Infantry, Company A, Civil War Collection, Military Collection, Box 72, Folder 12, State Archives of North Carolina, Raleigh, NC.

[17] John W. Moore, *Roster of North Carolina Troops in the War Between the States* (Raleigh, NC: Ashe & Gatling, 1882), 121.

[18] James Hall Wood Company Muster Rolls, RG 109, Carded Records Showing Military Service of Soldiers Who Fought in Confederate Organizations, NARA.

When recounting the engagement at Cool Spring in the regimental history of the 4th North Carolina Infantry, a fellow soldier said of Wood, "No better man died during the war than this splendid soldier. He was a Christian gentleman, a young man of much promise, and a model soldier; brave, gallant, and faithful." Colonel Wood's remains were returned home, and now rest in the Third Creek Presbyterian Church Cemetery in Rowan County, North Carolina.[19]

5th Alabama Infantry

S.R. Burnett (private)

Private S.R. Burnett enlisted as a private in Company C, 5th Alabama Infantry. He was mortally wounded during the Battle of Cool Spring. He died on July 21, at the General Hospital in Winchester from a breast wound. The location of his remains is unknown.[20]

George W. Prude (private)

Days after the opening shots of the Civil War, eighteen-year-old George W. Prude enlisted in Company H, 5th Alabama Infantry on April 20, 1861. Two of his brothers, David and Jesse, also offered their services to the Confederate army. Before enlisting, George worked on his father's cotton farm in Pickens County, which in 1860 counted twenty-two enslaved people.[21] George Prude received a $50 bounty upon enlistment. Between July 28 and October 25, 1863, Prude was hospitalized at General Hospital No. 9 in Richmond for an unknown reason. In the spring of 1864, Prude was again hospitalized for an undisclosed malady. He returned to duty on June 17, 1864. He was killed in action at Cool Spring. He is buried in Stonewall Confederate Cemetery in Winchester. His father filed a death claim on November 15, 1864.[22]

---

[19] Walter Clark, *Histories of the Several Regiments and Battalions from North Carolina in the Great War 1861-'65* (Raleigh, NC: E.M. Uzell, 1901), 1: 260.
[20] S.R. Burnett, 5th Alabama Infantry, CSR, NARA.
[21] 1860 U.S. Census-Slave Schedule, Johnathan Prude, May 3, 2020, Ancestry.com.
[22] George W. Prude, 5th Alabama Infantry, CSR, NARA.

Daniel C. Rankin (private)
On July 29, 1861, Monroe, Alabama, resident Daniel C. Rankin enlisted in Company C (old Company D), 5th Alabama Infantry at Bells Landing. He mustered into service on September 25, 1861. Rankin left his job as a farm laborer and joined his younger brother, Duncan, who enlisted in March 1861 in the same regiment.[23] In January 1864, Daniel, his brother Duncan, and Sergeant William A. Dudley approached their regimental commander, Captain T.M. Riley, and offered to reenlist unconditionally for the duration of the war. Captain Riley relayed this news to brigade commander Cullen A. Battle. Battle used this gesture to rally other soldiers to take similar action; his was the first brigade to re-enlist unconditionally for the war.[24] Daniel Rankin was killed in action during the Battle of Cool Spring. He is buried in Stonewall Confederate Cemetery in Winchester, Virginia. His brother, Duncan, was captured on April 2, 1865, in Petersburg and imprisoned at Point Lookout, Maryland. He was released on June 7, 1865.[25]

6th Alabama Infantry

Elkanah G. Arant (private)
A resident of Lowndes County, Alabama, Elkanah G. Arant left his family farm at the age of seventeen and enlisted in Company M, 6th Alabama Infantry on March 1, 1862.[26] He was paid a $50 bounty upon enlistment. On May 15, 1862, shortly after his enlistment, Arant was admitted to CSA General Hospital in Danville, Virginia, for rubeola. He returned to duty on July 16. Regimental muster rolls from October indicate he was "sick in Richmond since Aug. 30." On May 2, 1863, Private Arant was wounded during the Battle of Chancellorsville. He was treated for gunshot wounds to the thigh and perineum at Moore Hospital in Richmond, Virginia. He was transferred on May 28 to the 3rd Alabama Hospital to convalesce. The hospital granted him a sixty-day furlough on July 25, 1863. Arant

---

[23] 1860 U.S. Census, Monroe, Alabama, Daniel Rankin, April 25, 2020, Ancestry.com.
[24] B.F. Riley, *Makers and Romance of Alabama History* (United States: Good Press, 2019), 245.
[25] Daniel C. Rankin, 5th Alabama Infantry, CSR, NARA.
[26] 1860 U.S. Census, Southern Division, Lowndes, Alabama, Elkanah Arant, May 7, 2020, Ancestry.com.

was mortally wounded during the Battle of Cool Spring. June and July 1864 muster rolls list Arant as "wounded 18 July 64 and sent to hospital." Muster rolls from September and October indicate he was "absent, wounded July 18 and supposed to be dead." Arant is buried in a grave mistakenly marked "E.G. Arans" at Stonewall Confederate Cemetery in Winchester. His date of death is recorded as July 21, 1864.[27]

9th Louisiana Infantry

Reuben Allen Pierson (captain)

William H. Pierson of Bienville, Louisiana, owned one of the largest plantations in the parish, cultivating over 150 acres of crops and 490 acres of timber.[28] Ten people were enslaved on his plantation in 1850.[29] Four of Pierson's nine sons offered their service to the Confederacy; among them was Reuben Allen Pierson. Born in 1834, Reuben Pierson attended Mt. Lebanon University and was working as a school teacher in Bienville Parish when the Civil War began.[30] Pierson enlisted for a term of one year in Company C, 9th Louisiana Infantry on July 7, 1861. Pierson spent several weeks at Camp Moore, where he "gained a great reputation with all the boys who have been placed under my charge as guards."[31] On August 14, 1861, shortly after arriving in Virginia, Pierson was hospitalized for typhoid fever. He returned to duty on October 20.[32] He was appointed sergeant on December 28, 1861. On February 5, 1862, Pierson reenlisted for the duration of the war. He was elected captain on April 15, 1862. Muster rolls between July and September 1863 marked Pierson "Present in arrest or confinement." Writing to his father on July 15, Pierson explained: "My Col. arrested me because one of the men crossed over the fense [sic] into the field with his gun to get around a mudhole...I have applied for a trial and honorable acquittal which I

---

27 Elkanah G. Arant, 6th Alabama Infantry, CSR, NARA.

28 Thomas W. Cutrer and T. Michael Parrish, eds. *Brothers in Grey: The Civil War Letters of the Pierson Family* (Baton Rouge: Louisiana State University Press, 1997), 2.

29 1850 U.S. Census-Slave Schedule, William H Pierson, May 9, 2020, Ancestry.com.

30 Cutrer and Parrish, eds. *Brothers in Grey*, 8.

31 Ibid., 29.

32 Reuben Allen Pierson to James F. Pierson, October 20, 2861, in ibid., 255.

hope to attain soon."[33] The charges were eventually dropped and the matter resolved by November 1863. On May 5, 1864, Pierson was wounded during the Battle of the Wilderness. He was admitted to General Hospital No. 4 in Richmond on May 7 and treated for a gunshot wound to the right hand. On May 10, he was furloughed for thirty days to recover at a relative's home in Thomasville, Georgia.[34] He returned to duty with the 9th Louisiana on July 16. On the morning of July 18, Pierson was assigned command of a skirmish line on the west bank of the Shenandoah River near Castleman's Ferry; Union soldiers were hidden among the trees and bushes on the opposite bank of the river. Warning shots from the east bank prompted Pierson's command to fall to the ground and take cover. Pierson, however, did not take cover and instead "walked along perfectly regardless of dangers and exclaimed 'Boys see those Yankees... shoot them.'"[35] Shortly after he uttered those words Pierson was shot through his right arm, just below the shoulder. The ball went through his side and lodged in his clothes on the opposite side. Philip Collins, Pierson's cousin and comrade in the 9th Louisiana, wrote Pierson's father: "He only spoke twice after he fell. He spoke to me and sayed [sic] he was killed dead to take him out and he died immediately...We had a coffin made for him. He was buried in the grave yard of Mr. P.D. Shepherd near Berryville."[36] Pierson was reinterred in Stonewall Confederate Cemetery in Winchester, Virginia. In a postscript to Collins' letter, fellow Confederate F.A. Bledsoe eulogized Pierson as "a brave officer & much beloved by his company. He was true as steel—good and kind to his men. His bravery suited him well for the battlefield... His loss is felt greatly."[37]

12th Alabama Infantry

John T. Eberhart (private)

---

[33] Reuben Allen Pierson to William H. Pierson, July 15, 1863 in Cutrer and Parrish, eds. *Brothers in Grey*, 202.

[34] Reuben Allen Pierson, 9th Louisiana Infantry, CSR, NARA.

[35] Philip L. Collins to William H. Pierson, July 28, 1864 in Cutrer and Parrish, eds., *Brothers in Grey*, 241-242.

[36] Philip L. Collins to William H. Pierson, July 28, 1864 in ibid., 241.

[37] Ibid., 242.

John T. Eberhart worked as a farmer in Fredonia, Alabama, at the outset of the Civil War.[38] One of his few surviving Civil War service records indicates he was mustered into Company F, 12th Alabama Infantry on March 2, 1863, for the duration of the war. He was listed as present on company muster rolls between April and June 1864.[39] Eberhart was killed at Cool Spring. Captain Thomas Park, 12th Alabama, wrote of Eberhart's death: "Private Eberheart [sic], of my company, was instantly killed...When Eberheart was killed, Private Tom K--- called me earnestly to him and amid a heavy shower of bullets, I went to him... I took care of his pocket-book, his wife's ambrotype, and bible, and will send them to her at Fredonia, Alabama, the first opportunity. [Eberhart] was a brave, uncomplaining, good soldier sent to my company as a conscript."[40] The location of Eberhart's burial is unknown.

Alexander Majors (lieutenant)

A farmer from DeKalb County, Alabama, Alexander Majors enlisted in the 12th Alabama Infantry on June 13, 1861. Majors was twenty years old at the time of his enlistment. At the Battle of South Mountain, on September 14, 1862, Majors was captured. Evidence indicates that he spent time at Fort Delaware prison until exchanged on November 10, 1862. During the Battle of Chancellorsville, Majors suffered a wound to his right hand. By the time of the Battle of Cool Spring, Majors held the rank of lieutenant.[41] During the fighting on July 18, 1864, Lieutenant Majors was mortally wounded when a "Minnie ball had cut his artery in his leg." Captain Robert Park, who was by Majors' side at the moment he was wounded described Majors' mortal wounding: "Lieutenant Majors and I were running near each other in quick pursuit of the enemy, when he exclaimed that he was shot, but continued to run for some distance, and then suddenly fell. I stopped by his side and offered him some water from my canteen, which he hastily drank, and then sank down and instantly expired... Majors had been but

---

[38] 1860 U.S. Census, Northern Division, Chambers, Alabama, John T. Eberhart, May 7, 2020, Ancestry.com.
[39] J.T. Eberhart, 12th Alabama Infantry, CSR, NARA.
[40] Robert E. Park, "Diary of Robert E. Park, Macon, GA, Late Captain Twelfth Alabama Regiment, Confederate States Army" *Southern Historical Society Papers* I, no. 5 (1876): 386.
[41] Alexander Majors, 12th Alabama Infantry, CSR, NARA.

recently promoted, and was an officer of decided promise."[42] Although reportedly buried in Massanutten Cemetery in Woodstock, Virginia, no grave marker for him exists in that cemetery. Majors could be buried in the unknown section of the Stonewall Confederate Cemetery in Winchester, Virginia. A marker for Majors in DeKalb County, Alabama, notes simply that he is "buried in VA."[43]

G.W. Parnell (private)

Few service records survive to detail the service of G.W. Parnell. He served in Company C, 12th Alabama Infantry during the Battle of Cool Spring. He received a mortal gunshot wound to his chest and was taken to the General Hospital in Winchester, Virginia. He died on July 21, 1864.[44] He is most likely buried in Stonewall Confederate Cemetery in Winchester in a grave marked "G.R. Purnell."[45]

Jasper West (private)

The historical record of Private Jasper West is sparse and lacking; his service records include merely two entries: he served in Company E, 12th Alabama Infantry and suffered a gunshot wound to his head during the Battle of Cool Spring. He was admitted to the General Hospital in Winchester on July 20 and died on July 23. He is most likely buried in Stonewall Confederate Cemetery in a grave erroneously marked "Joseph West."[46]

12th Georgia Infantry

William F. Lowe (lieutenant)

William F. Lowe enlisted in Company F, 12th Georgia Infantry on June 11, 1861, in Drayton, Georgia. Lowe was wounded at Sharpsburg (the Battle of Antietam) on September 17, 1862. On December 19, 1862, Lowe was elected lieutenant. He was "mentioned for gallantry" for actions during the Battle of Chancellorsville on May

---

42 Park, "Diary of Robert E. Park," 386.
43 Alexander Majors, July 8, 2020, findagrave.com.
44 G.W. Parnell, 12th Alabama Infantry, CSR, NARA.
45 This grave references a soldier in Company C, 12th Alabama with the same death date (July 21, 1864) as G.W. Parnell.
46 Jasper West, 12th Alabama Infantry, CSR, NARA.

2 and 3, 1863. Lowe suffered a gunshot wound to his foot on May 16, 1864. The circumstances surrounding his wounding are unknown. He spent a week recovering at Jackson Hospital in Richmond and was transferred to Macon, Georgia, to recuperate. He returned to his unit in early summer. He was killed in action during the Battle of Cool Spring. The location of his remains are unknown.[47]

21st Georgia Infantry

Samuel Godwin (private)

Thirty-four-year-old Samuel Godwin resided with his mother and two younger relatives on his Montgomery County farm before enlisting and being mustered into service with Company G, 21st Georgia Infantry on October 23, 1863, in Macon.[48] He was present on company muster rolls between December 1863 and June 1864. He was killed in action during the Battle of Cool Spring. His mother filed a death claim on November 1, 1864, swearing in an affidavit from Montgomery County, Georgia, that as Godwin had no wife, no children, and no father, she had legal claim to "whatever may have been due [Samuel Godwin] at the time of his death for pay, bounty or other allowances for his services as Private."[49] The location of his remains is unknown.

26th Georgia Infantry

David J. Hickox (private)

David J. Hickox enlisted in Company H, 3rd Regiment Georgia Infantry on March 1, 1862, for the duration of the war. After enlistment, Hickox received a $50 bounty. The twenty-two-year-old farmer was married and had two daughters.[50] In the fall of 1862, Hickox was hospitalized at Winder Hospital in Richmond for several weeks. Hickox was transferred to Company C, 26th Georgia Infantry on April 10, 1863. He was killed in action at the Battle of

---

[47] William F. Lowe, 32nd North Carolina Infantry, CSR, NARA.

[48] 1860 U.S. Census, Montgomery, Georgia, Samuel Godwin, May 4, 2020, Ancestry.com.

[49] Samuel Godwin, 21st Georgia Infantry, CSR, NARA.

[50] 1860 U.S. Census, Ware, Georgia, David Heecox, April 25, 2020, Ancestry.com.

Cool Spring and is buried in Stonewall Confederate Cemetery in Winchester, Virginia.[51]

Stephen W. Myers (sergeant)
Stephen W. Myers, a resident of Ware County, Georgia, enlisted in Company L, 26th Georgia Infantry on May 4, 1861, at Tybee Island.[52] At the time of the Battle of Cool Spring, he held the rank of ordnance sergeant. Myers was mortally wounded during the battle and died on July 20, 1864 in a field hospital. The whereabouts of his remains are unknown.[53]

Bryant Sweat (sergeant)
Born in 1839, Ware County resident Bryant Sweat left his prosperous family farm which utilized the enslaved labor of fourteen people, and enlisted in Company E, 26th Georgia Infantry on April 18, 1861.[54] By July 1861 Sweat attained the rank of sergeant. Sweat was admitted to the CSA General Hospital in Farmville, Virginia, on June 10, 1863, to be treated for "intermittent fever." He was released on June 30, 1863, and sent to the defenses of Richmond. During the Battle of Cool Spring, Sweat was shot in the chest. The wound was mortal; he died July 21 at the General Hospital in Winchester. He is buried in Stonewall Confederate Cemetery.[55]

30th North Carolina Infantry

Arkin B. Bell (private)
Born in 1835, Arkin Bell enlisted in Company I, 30th North Carolina Infantry on March 10, 1862. The Black Creek, North Carolina, resident worked as a carpenter prior to his military service.[56] On September 16, 1862, he was admitted to Chimborazo Hospital #3 to

---

[51] David J. Hickox, 26th Georgia Infantry, CSR, NARA.

[52] Alfred C. Young, III, ed., *The Complete Roster and Service Records of Lee's Army of Northern Virginia During the Overland Campaign* (Baton Rouge: Louisiana State University Press, 2019), 1735.

[53] Stephen W. Myers, 26th Georgia Infantry, CSR, NARA.

[54] 1860 U.S. Census-Slave Schedule, James A. Sweat, May 2, 2020, Ancestry.com.

[55] Bryant Sweat, 26th Georgia Infantry, CSR, NARA.

[56] William Thomas Venner, *The 30th North Carolina Infantry in the Civil War* (Jefferson, NC: McFarland, 2018), 377.

be treated for pneumonia. He was given a sixty-day furlough to recover; his furlough expired on November 12, 1862. Bell was marked "absent at home without leave" on the company's muster roll at the end of December 1862. In March 1863, having been declared "unfit for active field service," Bell was assigned to hospital duty at the General Hospital in Wilson, North Carolina. After being examined at the hospital, the Medical Board unanimously declared "said private is not diseased as he claims to be, but is competent for the active duties of a soldier." Medical Director William A. Carrington further commented that the delay in this examination was caused by the fact that several other soldiers had been sent to him for hospital duty, and were also found competent for active service. Bell was marked "absent without leave" on the company's April-July 1863 muster roll.[57] At the Battle of Cool Spring, Private Bell was "mangled to death by a direct hit from an artillery shell."[58] The location of Bell's remains is unknown.

John N. Black (sergeant)

At the age of twenty, John N. Black enlisted in the 30th North Carolina Infantry on September 13, 1861. He was killed at Cool Spring. The whereabouts of his remains is unknown.[59]

Elijah Crotts (private)

Elijah Crotts was conscripted into service with Company H, 30th North Carolina Infantry on August 27, 1863, in Cleveland County, North Carolina. Born in 1822, he married Rachel Self in December 1851.[60] He was killed in action during the Battle of Cool Spring. The location of his remains is unknown.

Aaron Leonidas DeArmond (sergeant)

Born in Mecklenburg, North Carolina, on February 12, 1827, Aaron DeArmond was married with four children (a fifth was born during the war) when the Civil War began.[61] He left his farm and enlisted

---

[57] Arkin B. Bell, 30th North Carolina Infantry, CSR, NARA.

[58] Venner, *The 30th North Carolina Infantry*, 199.

[59] John N. Black, 30th North Carolina Infantry, CSR, NARA.

[60] Elijah Crotts Marriage License, December 7, 1851, North Carolina County Registers of Deeds, Record Group 048, North Carolina State Archives, Raleigh, NC.

[61] 1860 U.S. Census, Eastern Division, Mecklenburg, North Carolina, Aaron

in Company K, 30th North Carolina Infantry on September 13, 1861. He was promoted to third sergeant on September 27, before being mustered into the regiment on October 8, 1861. DeArmond was captured at the Battle of Antietam. He was exchanged and returned to the regiment by early December. DeArmond was wounded at the Battle of Fredericksburg.[62] He was admitted to Winder Hospital (Richmond) on December 17, 1862, and transferred to Danville General Hospital on December 28. Writing home to his wife, DeArmond recalled, "I was struck by a [bullet] which cracked my arm...4 inches from my shoulder."[63] He returned to duty with his regiment on January 17, 1863. On November 7, 1863, DeArmond was captured at Kelly's Ford. He was sent to Point Lookout Prison and was exchanged on March 17, 1864. During the Battle of Cool Spring, DeArmond was "mutilated by shrapnel."[64] He was admitted to CSA General Hospital in Charlottesville on July 25. He was transferred to General Hospital No. 9 in Richmond on July 31, 1864. Deemed well enough to be discharged, DeArmond was given a furlough to return home to recover from his wounds. During his journey home, his condition worsened. Less than three miles from his home but unable to continue his trip, he took shelter for the night in a chicken coop and died.[65] He is buried in Sardis Presbyterian Church Cemetery in Charlotte, North Carolina.

Richard Felton (corporal)

Richard Felton was a twenty-nine-year-old farmer when he enlisted in Company F, 30th North Carolina Infantry on August 31, 1861.[66] The Tarboro resident spent November and December 1861 at home on sick furlough. In March 1862, Felton was promoted to corporal and was absent from his unit on recruiting service. He was wounded in battle at Malvern Hill on July 1, 1862, and sent home to convalesce.

DeArmond, May 4, 2020, Ancestry.com.

[62] Aaron DeArmond Diary quoted in Martha R. Brown, *Holding Sweet Communion* (United States: CreateSpace, 2012), 203.

[63] Letter of Aaron DeArmond, January 12, 1863, quoted in Venner, *The 30th North Carolina*, 75.

[64] Letter of Aaron DeArmond, January 12, 1863, quoted in ibid., 199.

[65] Aaron Leonidas DeArmond, Charlotte Museum of History Exhibit "Mecklenburg Soldiers," May 4, 2020, Ancestry.com.

[66] Venner, *The 30th North Carolina*, 348.

Corporal Felton was killed in action during the Battle of Cool Spring. The location of his remains is unknown.[67]

Thomas Gupton (private)
Thomas Gupton worked as a farm laborer in Louisburg, North Carolina, before he enlisted in Company I, 30th North Carolina Infantry on September 10, 1861. The twenty-one-year-old was plagued by illness throughout much of his service. Between June 2 and 11, 1862, Gupton was hospitalized for chronic diarrhea. Unit muster rolls indicate he was absent at home without leave August–December 1862. In April 1863 he was hospitalized at Moore Hospital in Richmond for *debilitas*. He was then transferred to a Danville hospital and treated for lumbago. He returned to active duty on June 16, 1863. Between November and December 1863, Private Gupton was in General Hospital No. 7 in Raleigh, North Carolina, for reasons not indicated on muster rolls.[68] During the Battle of Cool Spring, Gupton was "mangled to death by a direct hit from a Union artillery shell."[69] The whereabouts of his remains is unknown.

James W. Teachey (sergeant)
Twenty-three-year-old day laborer James W. Teachey enlisted in Company E, 30th North Carolina Infantry on August 28, 1861. The Duplin County, North Carolina, resident was married.[70] Teachey was promoted to sergeant on June 1, 1863. In late May 1864 he was admitted to Chimborazo Hospital in Richmond and treated for diarrhea. He returned to duty on June 17, 1864. Teachey was killed in action during the Battle of Cool Spring. The whereabouts of his remains is unknown. His younger brother, Jacob, who also fought with Company E, 30th North Carolina, "took chunks of shrapnel through his bowels" during the battle.[71] Jacob died on January 17, 1865.

Louis Redmon Wells (corporal)
Tarboro, North Carolina, resident Louis Redmon Wells enlisted in

---

[67] Richard Felton, 30th North Carolina Infantry, CSR, NARA.
[68] Thomas Gupton, 30th North Carolina, CSR, NARA.
[69] Venner, *The 30th North Carolina*, 199.
[70] *Wilmington Journal*, March 30, 1855.
[71] Venner, *The 30th North Carolina*, 199.

Company F, 30th North Carolina Infantry on August 31, 1861. The forty-six-year-old miller was married with six children.[72] Wells was promoted to sergeant on March 10, 1862. His rank was reduced to private in January 1864. At the time of the Battle of Cool Spring, Wells held the rank of corporal. During the battle Wells had "a minie bullet punch its way through his chest."[73] He died three days later, on July 21, 1864, in Winchester. The location of his remains is unknown.[74]

32nd North Carolina Infantry

Nicholas G. Long (private)
Nicholas G. Long was born in Mississippi in 1839. In 1860, he was working as a mechanic in Franklin County, North Carolina.[75] He enlisted in Company L, 15th North Carolina Infantry on May 20, 1861, in Louisburg. He mustered into service on June 30, 1861. He was wounded slightly during the Battle of Malvern Hill. On July 4, 1862, he was transferred to Company K, 32nd North Carolina Infantry. Private Long spent the early months of 1864 absent from his unit, marked "sick in hospital." On March 30, he was admitted to Jackson Hospital in Richmond to be treated for pneumonia. He was transferred to the North Carolina Hospital near Petersburg, Virginia, on April 11, with the strict directive that he "will report to the Surg. in charge or be considered a deserter." Muster rolls indicate he followed these orders. He was killed in action during the Battle of Cool Spring. The location of his remains is unknown.[76]

Gilbert M. Sherrill (captain)
Born on July 4, 1837, in Newton, North Carolina, Gilbert Milligan Sherrill was married and worked as a merchant when the Civil War began. According to the 1860 census he enslaved four people.[77] He

---

[72] 1860 U.S. Census, Edgecombe, North Carolina, April 25, 2020, Ancestry.com.

[73] Venner, *The 30th North Carolina*, 198.

[74] Louis Redmon Wells, 30th North Carolina Infantry, CSR, NARA.

[75] 1860 U.S. Census, Franklin, North Carolina, Nicholas Long, May 2, 2020, Ancestry.com.

[76] Nicholas G. Long, 15th North Carolina Infantry and 32nd North Carolina Infantry, CSR, NARA.

[77] 1860 U.S. Census-Slave Schedule, Gilbert M. Sherrill, April 30, 2020,

enlisted in Company E, 1st Battalion North Carolina Infantry on August 14, 1861. He was appointed second lieutenant upon enlistment. In April 1862, at Drewry's Bluff, Virginia, the 1st Battalion North Carolina Infantry was reorganized into the 32nd North Carolina Infantry.[78] Sherrill was promoted to lieutenant on May 1, 1862. On July 9, 1862, he was promoted to captain. In September and October, Captain Sherrill was "under arrest by orders of Lt. Col Williams." Specific details surrounding the reasons for his arrest are unknown. He returned to his regiment by November and no further disciplinary action appears in his service record. During the fight on the late afternoon of July 2, 1863, at Gettysburg, Sherrill was wounded. He was sent home on furlough and returned to his unit in September. During the Battle of Cool Spring he was shot in the shoulder. The wound proved mortal. Sherrill died at the General Hospital in Winchester on July 24. He is buried in Stonewall Confederate Cemetery in Winchester.[79]

<h3 align="center">36th Virginia Infantry</h3>

John T. Kimberling (sergeant)
Bland County laborer John T. Kimberling enlisted in Company G, 36th Virginia (2nd Kanawha Infantry) on May 3, 1862, in Dublin, Virginia. The twenty-one-year-old was appointed corporal upon enlistment. At the time of the Battle of Cool Spring, Kimberling held the rank of sergeant. He was "killed in action with the enemy" during the Battle of Cool Spring. He is buried at Stonewall Confederate Cemetery in Winchester.[80]

John T. Meadows (private)
John Meadows, a native of Mercer County, Virginia (now West Virginia), enlisted in Company I, 36th Virginia Infantry on December 10, 1862. Meadows enlisted as a private for the duration of the war.[81] According to the account of the Battle of Cool Spring in

---

Ancestry.com.

[78] For a general history of this regiment see John C. Rigdon *Historical Sketch and Roster of the North Carolina 32nd Infantry Regiment* (United States: Eastern Digital Resources, 2019).

[79] Gilbert M. Sherrill, 32nd North Carolina Infantry, CSR, NARA.

[80] John T. Kimberling, 36th Virginia Infantry, CSR, NARA.

[81] John T. Meadows, Company Muster Rolls, RG 109, Carded Records

the regimental history of the 36th Virginia Infantry, "The federals attempted to cross the gap on July 18 and were pushed back by the Southerners. During the fighting that day, two members of the 36th Virginia were killed, John Kimberling and John T. Meadows."[82] "He is buried in Stonewall Confederate Cemetery in a grave mistakenly marked "J.B. Meadows."

38th Georgia Infantry

Andrew Jackson "Jack" Williamson, Jr. (sergeant)
Andrew Jackson "Jack" Williamson, Jr. was one of twenty children of prominent Montgomery County resident Andrew Jackson Williamson, who served in the Georgia House of Representatives between 1853 and 1854.[83] Born in 1842, Jack worked on his family farm before he enlisted in Company C, 38th Georgia Infantry on October 1, 1861, in Augusta, Georgia, for the duration of the war. He was promoted to corporal on December 15, 1862. He was reported "absent-sick" on March and April 1863 muster rolls and subsequently treated for chronic bronchitis at General Hospital No. 21 in Richmond between May 10-27, when he was transferred to Chimborazo Hospital. He returned to duty with his regiment by July 1863. He was promoted to sergeant in January 1864. Williamson was killed in action during the Battle of Cool Spring. He is buried in Stonewall Confederate Cemetery in Winchester. His tombstone reads "J.W. Williamson."[84]

43rd North Carolina Infantry

William Beavans (lieutenant)
After William Beavans' six-month enlistment in the 1st North Carolina Infantry expired in early 1862, he enlisted in the 43rd North Carolina Infantry as a first sergeant on February 25, 1862. Two months after he enlisted in the regiment, Beavans was promoted to

---

Showing Military Service of Soldiers Who Fought in Confederate Organizations, NARA.
[82] J. L. Scott, *36th Virginia Infantry* (Lynchburg: H. E. Howard, 1987), 31.
[83] 1860 U.S. Census, Montgomery, Georgia, Andrew Jackson Williamson, May 4, 2020, Ancestry.com.
[84] Andrew Jackson Williamson, 38th Georgia Infantry, CSR, NARA.

second lieutenant. During the Battle of Cool Spring, Beavans was shot in the right leg. On the night of July 18, 1864, surgeons amputated Beavans' right leg and then sent him to a hospital in Winchester.[85] On the day Beavans died, July 31, 1864, he informed Kate Shepherd, a young woman from Winchester who had been nursing him, that he wanted "to get well for the sake of my parents" and that he "would love to see them."[86] Beavans is interred in the Stonewall Confederate Cemetery in Winchester.

Lieutenant William Beavans' tombstone in the
Stonewall Confederate Cemetery
(*Photo by Jonathan A. Noyalas*)

Marmaduke N. Bell (sergeant)

Edgecombe County farmer Marmaduke Bell enlisted in Company F, 43rd North Carolina Infantry on February 4, 1862. He was twenty-six years old at the time of enlistment. He mustered into service on April 2, 1862. Bell was promoted to corporal on July 26, 1862. By July 1864 Bell had attained the rank of sergeant. He was killed in action during the Battle of Cool Spring. He left behind a wife and three children.[87] He is buried in Lawrence Cemetery in Edgecombe

---

[85] William Beavans, 43rd North Carolina Infantry, CSR, NARA.

[86] Quoted in Manly Wade Wellman, *Rebel Boast: First at Bethel—Last at Appomattox* (New York: Henry Holt and Company, 1956), 190.

[87] 1860 U.S. Census, Eastern Division, Halifax, North Carolina, Marmaduke

Country, North Carolina.[88] His memorial marker incorrectly notes the year of his death as 1964.

Charles M. Bullard (private)

Charles M. Bullard served in Company H, 43rd North Carolina Infantry. Few of his service records exist. A surviving muster roll dated December 31, 1863-August 31, 1864, indicates he was "killed dead on the 18th of July 1864. Bounty done." The location of his remains is unknown.[89]

Illy N. Dicken (private)

Born around 1830, Illy Dicken worked as a farmer in Halifax County prior to enlisting in Company F, 43rd North Carolina Infantry on February 11, 1862. He mustered into service on April 2, 1862, and was present on all company muster rolls for the duration of his service. He was killed in action during the Battle of Cool Spring. The location of his remains is unknown.[90]

Edmund Jacob Dickins (private)

E.J. Dickins resided in Halifax County and worked as an overseer. He was married with two children (a third child was born in 1864) when he enlisted in Company F, 43rd North Carolina on May 14, 1862.[91] He was twenty-seven at the time of his enlistment. He was marked present and accounted for during the duration of his service. Dickins was killed during the Battle of Cool Spring.[92] The location of his remains is unknown.

Stephen W. Ellerbe (lieutenant)

Stephen Ellerbe, a resident of Wadesboro, North Carolina, was married and raising two young children on his prosperous estate, which in 1860 included twenty-three enslaved people, when the twenty-four-year-old enlisted in Company I, 43rd North Carolina

---

N. Bell, April 27, 2020, Ancestry.com.

[88] Marmaduke Bell, 43rd North Carolina Infantry, CSR, NARA.

[89] Charles M. Bullard, 43rd North Carolina Infantry, CSR, NARA.

[90] Illy N. Dicken, 43rd North Carolina Infantry, CSR, NARA.

[91] 1860 U.S. Census, Western District, Halifax, North Carolina, E. J. Dickins, April 28, 2020, Ancestry.com.

[92] E.J. Dickins, 43rd North Carolina Infantry, CSR, NARA.

Infantry on May 9, 1862.[93] In May and June 1862 he was reported on muster rolls as absent without leave. He was again absent without leave in November and December 1862. He spent several weeks in August at the General Hospital in Danville, Virginia, undergoing treatment for *debilitas* and returned to duty on September 8, 1863. He was subsequently placed under arrest for his conduct during the Battle of Gettysburg. Court-martial documents indicate Ellerbe "left [the] field at an early stage of each day battle without proper authority." During his period of detainment, September 1863-January 19, 1864, Ellerbe was promoted to lieutenant (November, 5, 1863). Ellerbe was cleared of charges and returned to his unit. During the Battle of Cool Spring he was shot through the mouth. Two days after the battle he was taken to Winchester General Hospital and died there on July 31. He is buried in Stonewall Confederate Cemetery in Winchester, Virginia. His grave is incorrectly marked "S.W. Elerb."[94]

Henry T. Jones (private)
Eighteen-year-old Henry T. Jones, an Edgecombe County, North Carolina resident, enlisted in Company E, 43rd North Carolina Infantry on May 16, 1862. He spent the first few months of his service at home sick. He returned to duty in August 1862. Between May and June 1863, Jones was in a hospital in Petersburg, Virginia. He was then admitted to Episcopal Church Hospital in Williamsburg, Virginia, on June 22, 1863. He was treated for acute rheumatism and released to duty on July 2, 1863. He was killed in action during the Battle of Cool Spring. The location of his remains is unknown.[95]

William Eli Lewis (private)
William Eli Lewis, a native of Halifax, North Carolina, enlisted in Company D, 43rd North Carolina Infantry on February 12, 1862. He was twenty-four years old at the time of enlistment. He was noted as being absent from his regiment "in camp near Drewry's Bluff" in August 1862. Private Lewis died from wounds received during the

---

[93] 1860 U.S. Census-Slave Schedule, Stephen Ellerbe, April 27, 2020, Ancestry.com.
[94] Stephen Ellerbe, 43rd North Carolina Infantry, CSR, NARA.
[95] Henry T. Jones, 43rd North Carolina Infantry, CSR, NARA.

Battle of Cool Spring. The location of his remains is unknown.[96]

Elisha Dargan "E.D." Liles (corporal)
Elisha Dargan "E.D." Liles was born on February 23, 1841, in Anson County, North Carolina. His family enslaved thirteen people on their farm in Lilesville.[97] Liles enlisted in Company I, 43rd North Carolina Infantry on February 25, 1862. He mustered into service on April 2, 1862. He was present on all company muster rolls for the duration of his service. On July 20, 1863, he was promoted to corporal. Liles was killed in action during the Battle of Cool Spring. He is buried in Stonewall Confederate Cemetery in Winchester.[98]

James W. Loften (private)
James Loften enlisted in Company A, 43rd North Carolina Infantry on November 23, 1863. He was present on company muster rolls until he was killed in action during the Battle of Cool Spring. His burial location is unknown.[99]

Jesse Macon (lieutenant)
Jesse Macon was born in Halifax County, North Carolina. His father was a doctor and the family enslaved six people.[100] His younger brother, Henry, enlisted in Company F, 43rd North Carolina Infantry in February 1862.[101] Jesse Macon was twenty-four years old when he enlisted in Company F, 15th Mississippi Infantry on May 8, 1862, in Corinth. In October 1862, Macon was reported as "home sick left us at V-burg [Vicksburg] Miss in July." In March 1863 Macon was transferred to Company F, 43rd North Carolina Infantry. He was promoted from private to lieutenant on June 1, 1863. Macon was wounded July 3, 1863, during the Battle of Gettysburg. Macon was mortally wounded at the Battle of Cool Spring. He is incorrectly reported on company muster rolls as being killed on July 20. The death claim filed August 29, 1864 by his father, Henry, reports Macon died on August 25 from "wounds received near Winchester

---

[96] William Eli Lewis, 43rd North Carolina Infantry, CSR, NARA.

[97] 1860 U.S. Census-Slave Schedule, Sanford Liles, May 2, 2020, Ancestry.com.

[98] Elisha D. Liles, 43rd North Carolina Infantry, CSR, NARA.

[99] James W. Loften, 43rd North Carolina Infantry, CSR, NARA.

[100] 1860 U.S. Census-Slave Schedule, Henry Macon, April 27, 2020, Ancestry.com.

[101] Henry A. Macon, 43rd North Carolina Infantry, CSR, NARA.

on the 18th of July."[102] He is buried near his brother Henry, who was killed in action on April 18, 1864, in Alston Cemetery in Halifax County, North Carolina.

John A. Pairman (private)

John A. Pairman (often appearing as Pearman) immigrated to the United States from Lanarkshire, Scotland, in May 1848. He married Temperance Harlow in Halifax County, North Carolina, on October 27, 1855. Their daughter, Marian, was born in 1859. John was working as a farmer when, at the age of thirty-three, he enlisted in Company F, 43rd North Carolina Infantry on February 10, 1862.[103] Pairman was killed in action at the Battle of Cool Spring. The location of his remains is unknown.

Andrew Parks (corporal)

Andrew Parks resided in Enfield, North Carolina, and worked as a farm overseer prior to enlisting in Company D, 43rd North Carolina Infantry on February 3, 1862. The thirty-seven-year-old Halifax County resident was married with two children.[104] He was mustered into service on April 2, 1862, and promoted to corporal in October 1862. During the early months of 1864, Parks was on detached service recruiting for the regiment. He was killed in action during the Battle of Cool Spring. The location of his remains is unknown.[105]

Joseph W. Phifer (corporal)

Joseph W. Phifer, a farmer from Wadesboro, North Carolina, enlisted in the 43rd North Carolina Infantry on February 25, 1862. He was twenty-three years old at the time of enlistment. He mustered into Company K on April 2, 1862. Shortly thereafter, between May and June 1862, Phifer was absent from the regiment on sick leave. On August 1, 1862, Phifer was promoted to corporal. He was reduced in rank to private on May 30, 1863. On March 30, 1864, he was again promoted to corporal. Joseph Phifer was killed in action during the

---

[102] Jesse Macon, 43rd North Carolina Infantry, CSR, NARA.
[103] 1860 U.S. Census, Western District, Halifax, North Carolina, John Pearman, April 27, 2020, Ancestry.com.
[104] 1860 U.S. Census, Eastern Division, Halifax, North Carolina, Andrew Parks, April 28, 2020, Ancestry.com.
[105] Andrew Parks, 43rd North Carolina Infantry, CSR, NARA.

Battle of Cool Spring. The location of his remains is unknown.[106]

William J. Smith (private)

Seventeen-year-old Anson County resident William J. Smith enlisted in Company H, 43rd North Carolina Infantry on May 2, 1862, at Camp Caswell. He was marked present, but "sick" on company muster rolls dated May-June 1863. He suffered a gunshot wound to his right foot on July 1, 1863, at Gettysburg and later captured. Smith was sent to DeCamp General Hospital on David's Island, New York, on July 17. He was paroled and exchanged at City Point, Virginia, on September 8, 1863. That same day, Smith was admitted to the General Hospital in Petersburg, where he received treatment for his foot injury. He was given a forty-day furlough on September 16, 1863. He returned to his unit by January 1864. He was "killed dead" during the Battle of Cool Spring on July 18, 1864. The location of his remains is unknown.[107]

John Stearns (private)

John Stearns, a resident of Union County, North Carolina, enlisted in Company B, 43rd North Carolina Infantry on February 19, 1862. The thirty-one-year-old farmer was married with three children.[108] He mustered into service on April 2, 1862, and was listed on initial muster rolls as "in hospital." He was killed in action during the Battle of Cool Spring. The location of his remains is unknown.[109]

John H. Outlaw (private)

John Outlaw enlisted in Company A, 43rd North Carolina Infantry on April 22, 1862, in Kenansville, North Carolina. He was mustered into service as a private to serve for the duration of the conflict. Outlaw was absent from the regiment due to sickness between July 1863- October 1863 when he was admitted to a hospital in Richmond. He returned to his regiment in December of that year. On the company muster roll from the summer of 1864, Outlaw was listed as

---

[106] Joseph W. Phifer, 43rd North Carolina Infantry, CSR, NARA.

[107] William J. Smith, 43rd North Carolina Infantry, CSR, NARA

[108] 1860 U.S. Census, Union, North Carolina, John Stearns, April 25, 2020, Ancestry.com.

[109] John Stearns, 43rd North Carolina Infantry, CSR, NARA.

"Killed July 18, 64"—the date of the Battle of Cool Spring. The location of his remains is unknown.[110]

Thomas B. Harrington (private)

Thomas B. Harrington was conscripted into service with Company K, 43rd North Carolina Infantry on January 7, 1864, at Camp Holmes in Raleigh. He was paid a bounty upon his enlistment. He died on July 25, 1864, from wounds received at the Battle of Cool Spring.[111] He is buried in Stonewall Confederate Cemetery in Winchester.[112]

43rd Tennessee (Vaughn's Brigade)

Samuel Hugh Vincent (private)

Samuel Vincent enlisted in Company D, 43rd Tennessee Infantry on November 1, 1861, in Decatur, Tennessee. The farmer from Meigs County was married with six children. Company muster rolls reported Vincent "at home sick" between July 1862 and February 1863. He was marked "absent without leave" between March and June 1863.[113] The 43rd Tennessee was captured at Vicksburg, exchanged, and reorganized as mounted infantry. Attached to General John C. Vaughn's Brigade, the unit joined General Jubal Early in the Shenandoah Valley in the spring of 1864.[114] Muster rolls beyond August 1863 do not survive for Samuel Vincent. In 1903, Vincent's widow, Elizabeth, filed for a widow's pension. In a sworn affidavit, Robert Spradling claimed: "I further swear that I was a member of the same company and regiment was on the Battlefield with him at Snicker's Ford, V[irgini]a on the Shenandoah River July 18, 1864 saw him killed with cannon ball, helped carry him off battlefield and helped to bury him." Elizabeth Vincent was granted

---

[110] John H. Outlaw, Company Muster Rolls, RG 109, Carded Records Showing Military Service of Soldiers Who Fought in Confederate Organizations, NARA.

[111] Thomas B. Harrington, 43rd North Carolina Infantry, CSR, NARA.

[112] The date of death on record at the cemetery is August 1, 1864.

[113] Samuel Vincent, 43rd Tennessee Infantry, CSR, NARA.

[114] For additional information on this regiment see John C. Rigdon, *Historical Sketch and Roster of the Tennessee 43rd Infantry Regiment* (Georgia: Digital Resources, 2009).

a class four widow's pension on August 15, 1903.[115] Samuel Vincent is buried in Stonewall Confederate Cemetery in Winchester.

51st Virginia Infantry

Lemuel Allen (private)
During the first summer of the Civil War, Lemuel Allen, a day laborer from Carroll County, Virginia, left his wife, Nancy, and young son, William, and enlisted in Company B, 51st Virginia Infantry.[116] The twenty-two-year-old mustered into service on July 31, 1861, in Wytheville. He was given a fifteen-day furlough on December 24, 1862. He was reported "absent-sick" from his unit during the month of June 1863. He returned to duty in July and in late summer (August 23-September 5) was on detached service in Patrick County, Virginia. Allen was killed during the Battle of Cool Spring. He is buried in Stonewall Confederate Cemetery in Winchester in a grave incorrectly marked "Pvt Samuel Allen."[117]

53rd North Carolina Infantry

John F. Collins (sergeant)
Twenty-three-year-old John F. Collins enlisted in Company B, 53rd North Carolina Regiment in Dunn Hill, Virginia, on June 23, 1862. He was promoted to sergeant on December 1, 1863. He was reported as "absent on furlough" between January-February 1864. He was mortally wounded during the Battle of Cool Spring and died on July 21 at the General Hospital in Winchester. It is likely his remains are buried in Stonewall Confederate Cemetery in Winchester in a gravesite incorrectly identified to "S.F. Collins."[118]

William Allison Owens (colonel)
A twenty-seven-year-old attorney from Mecklenburg, North Carolina, William Allison Owens was commissioned a first

---

[115] Alabama, Texas, and Virginia Confederate Pensions, 1884-1958, Samuel Hugh Vincent, May 9, 2020, Ancestry.com.
[116] 1860 U.S. Census, Carroll, Virginia, Lemuel Allen, May 5, 2020, Ancestry.com.
[117] Lemuel Allen, 51st Virginia Infantry, CSR, NARA.
[118] John F. Collins, 2nd North Carolina Infantry, CSR, NARA.

lieutenant on April 16, 1861, in the 1st North Carolina Volunteer Infantry. He mustered out of the regiment on November 12, 1861. On January 28, 1862, Owens received a commission as a major in the 34th North Carolina Infantry. Owens remained in the 34th North Carolina until March 31, 1862, when he was promoted to lieutenant colonel in the 11th North Carolina Infantry. Slightly more than one month later, on May 6, 1862, Owens was commissioned colonel of the 53rd North Carolina Infantry. Owens received wounds to his middle finger and side at the Battle of Spotsylvania Court House on May 12, 1864. It took Colonel Owens more than two months to recover from those wounds.[119] Owens returned to his regiment on July 17, 1864, the day prior to his unit being engaged at the Battle of Cool Spring. Colonel James Morehead, who succeeded Owens in command of the regiment after Owens was mortally wounded at Cool Spring, wrote decades after the conflict that Colonel Owens returned "just as the regiment was eating dinner, and almost while we were congratulating him on his safe return." According to Morehead, Owens was struck in the bowels by a stray shot after the fighting subsided on the night of July 18. Owens died the following day.[120] Colonel Owens was initially buried in the Old Chapel Cemetery in Millwood, Virginia, but in 1867 his remains were moved to the Old Settlers Cemetery in Charlotte, North Carolina.[121]

William A. Shofner (private)
Eighteen-year-old William A. Shofner enlisted in Company F, 53rd North Carolina Infantry on April 18, 1864. His last name has several spellings on record (Shofner, Shoffner, Shaffner, Shufner). By enlisting in the regiment William joined his older brother, George, who enlisted in the regiment in 1862. William was reported "absent sick" on muster rolls dated throughout 1864. He was admitted to the General Hospital in Winchester on July 20. He succumbed to wounds received at Cool Spring on July 27, 1864.[122]

54th North Carolina Infantry

---

[119] William Allison Owens, 53rd North Carolina Infantry, CSR, NARA.
[120] Clark, ed., *Histories of Several Regiments and Battalions from North Carolina*, 3: 259.
[121] *Charlotte Democrat*, March 5, 1867.
[122] W.A. Shofner, 2nd North Carolina Infantry, CSR, NARA.

William B. Morrison (sergeant)
William B. Morrison was eighteen years old when he enlisted in Company H, 54th North Carolina Infantry on April 28, 1862. The farmer from Yadkin County, North Carolina, mustered into service on May 23, 1862. He received a $50 bounty upon his enlistment. On November 7, 1863, Morrison was captured at Rappahannock Station, Virginia. He was confined as a prisoner of war at Point Lookout, Maryland, on November 11, 1863. Sergeant Morrison was paroled at City Point, Virginia, on March 16, 1864, and exchanged on March 20. He was mortally wounded during the Battle of Cool Spring and died on July 22 at the General Hospital in Winchester.[123] He is buried in Stonewall Confederate Cemetery in Winchester in a grave marked "W.E. Morrison."

60th Virginia Infantry

Haywood Hodge (private)
Laborer Haywood Hodge of Grayson County, Virginia, was twenty-two years old at the time of his enlistment in the summer of 1861 in Company H, 60th Virginia Infantry in Princeton, Virginia (now West Virginia).[124] He was reported "absent with leave" on May 15, 1863. He returned to the unit by August 15, 1863, but lost three months' pay ($33.00). In August 1863 Hodge was cited for losing two cartridges, $0.30 per cartridge and docked $0.60 in pay. He was given a furlough on February 22, 1864, and returned to duty with his unit by April 15. During the Battle of Cool Spring, Hodge suffered a gunshot wound to his shoulder. He was hospitalized in Winchester and died of his wounds on July 20, 1864. He is buried at Stonewall Confederate Cemetery in Winchester, Virginia.[125]

61st Alabama Infantry

Robert Caswell Ellington (private)
Born in Georgia on December 10, 1845, Robert Caswell Ellington left

---

[123] William B. Morrison, 54th North Carolina Infantry, CSR, NARA.
[124] 1860 U.S. Census, Grayson, Virginia, Haywood Hodge, May 5, 2020, Ancestry.com.
[125] Haywood Hodge, 60th Virginia Infantry, CSR, NARA.

his family farm in Randolph County, Alabama, and enlisted in Company F, 61st Alabama Infantry on September 1, 1863. His father enslaved one female.[126] Just eighteen years old at the time of the Battle of Cool Spring, Ellington sustained a mortal wound on July 18. He died in Winchester on July 19. He is buried in Stonewall Confederate Cemetery in Winchester.

Thomas' Legion (North Carolina)

John A. Beck

In July 1862 Confederate authorities allowed William Holland Thomas to form a regiment of Cherokee and white soldiers that would act as a guerilla force to defend North Carolina from Union incursion. This unit became known as Thomas' Legion.[127] John Alvertes Beck enlisted in Company F, 1st Regiment Thomas' Legion North Carolina Troops on July 19, 1862, the day the company was officially organized. The twenty-eight-year-old farmer from Jackson County, North Carolina, was married with four children at the time of his enlistment.[128] He was on detached duty between September and October 1862. In the spring of 1864, a contingent of Thomas' Legion joined General Jubal Early's army in Virginia. Beck was among this group of men who left North Carolina for the Old Dominion. John A. Beck died on July 19, 1864, from wounds received during the Battle of Cool Spring.[129] He is buried in Stonewall Confederate Cemetery in Winchester.

---

[126] 1860 U.S. Census-Slave Schedule, Arch Ellington (William Archibald Ellington), May 2, 2020, Ancestry.com.

[127] For additional information about this unit see Clark, ed., *Histories of Several Regiments and Battalions from North Carolina*, 3: 729-761.

[128] 1860 U.S. Census, Jackson, North Carolina, John A. Beck, May 3, 2020, Ancestry.com.

[129] John A. Beck, Thomas' Legion, CSR, NARA.

"May Peace Soon be Restored"
The 1862 Diary of Ephraim Burket, 110th Pennsylvania

Cheyenne Nimes

The following excerpted diary entries are from the diary my great-great-grandfather Ephraim Burket kept during the 1862 Shenandoah Valley Campaign. At the time, Burket served as a hospital steward in the 110th Pennsylvania Volunteer Infantry. As a hospital steward Burket provided critical assistance to the regiment's medical staff. In addition to assisting regimental surgeons, hospital stewards needed to possess "knowledge of practical pharmacy," and be able to perform various minor medical procedures such as tooth extraction.[1] When Burket mustered into Company D, 110th Pennsylvania Volunteer Infantry, on December 19, 1861, he was thirty-one years old and married to Mary Harnish. At the time of his enlistment Ephraim and his wife, Mary, had two children, Lee Keller born in 1859 and Elmer born in 1861. The couple had a third child, Henry Clay born in 1863. After the war, the Burkets had three more children, Grace Hannah, John Warren, and Anna Kate.[2] At the Civil War's outset Ephraim and his family lived in Sinking Valley, Pennsylvania, located in the south central part of the state, on a farm William Penn sold "for 370 pounds, 12 shillings and 1 penny current money of Pennsylvania in specie, in addition to which said James Stuart was to pay a quit rent of one (1) peppercorn on the first day of March of each and every year thereafter, forever

---

[1] For additional discussion of the role of hospital stewards see George Worthington Adams, *Doctors in Blue: The Medical History of the Union Army in the Civil War* (Baton Rouge: Louisiana State University Press, 1980), 67.

[2] For further discussion of Burket's children see Theodore Blair Patton, *History of the Descendants of Peter Burket, Late of Sinking Valley, Blair County, Penna., Who Died Jan. 20, 1867* (Huntingdon, PA: Printed at State Reformatory, 1897), 21.

if demanded."[3]

The words Burket committed to his diary during the 1862 Valley Campaign reflect stoicism in the face of unimaginable horror. Additionally, Burket's diary offers important insight into movements and operations of Union troops in the Shenandoah Valley in the spring of 1862, provides perspective on the waging of war against civilian populations, reveals attitudes of Union soldiers toward slavery, and offers assessments of various figures with whom Burket interacted.

Beyond that, however, Burket's diary offers a candid glimpse into our nation's most tumultuous moment and the toll that combat and campaign takes on the human body. 160 years removed from the moment Burket enlisted in the 110th Pennsylvania Volunteer Infantry, some cannot shake the impulse to view the Civil War through a romantic lens. Ephraim Burket's diary is detailed, revealing, and candid. He recorded his thoughts not weeks or years later, but minutes or hours after the sulphureous odor of the battlefield lingered in his nose, as the limbs he assisted in amputating piled up, and as the screams of the dying filled the air. Throughout his diary Burket openly questioned the violence. That Ephraim fought for God and country was not his cliché, because he had no cliché. He had God and he had country, in that order. He is remembered now only because he left a diary behind. While Burket's name will never hold a place among the Civil War's most famous figures—Grant, Sherman, Sheridan, Lee, Jackson, and Stuart—Burket's diary and experiences in 1862 serve as a useful reminder that it is because of the millions of men such as him, those committed to the Union's preservation and slavery's destruction, that America exists—a nation united, one dedicated, as President Abraham Lincoln noted in the Gettysburg Address, "to the proposition that all men are created equal."[4]

March 2, Sunday, 1862

Quite cold but calm this morning. We found ourselves in the woods but all night for a fight. We got up and eat often and then thought that we must

---

[3] Patton, *History of the Descendants*, 3.
[4] John G. Nicolay and John Hay, *Complete Works of Abraham Lincoln* (New York: The Tandy-Thomas Co., 1905), 9: 209.

have some dinner. It commenced to snow at 10 oclock and snowed very fast and we commenced to build some brush pens to shelter us and we was getting fixed up quite comfortable and we got orders to march back to our old quarters again.[5] We was very much disappointed for we expected to go on to Winchester which we was very anxious to take and or that appeared to be the whole desire of the regiment. But at 3 oclock we took up the line of march to our old camp where we arrived at dusk although it was the Sabbath day. I thought that it was the longest day I ever passed. I am well on the Virginia soil 2 miles from Paw Paw. Our Gen Lander died at 4 ½ oclock in the afternoon and we are sorry that he has died as he was a brave man one that would lead an army into the Battlefield but he was our Major Gen of this Division of some 20 or 25000 under his control.[6] All men must die let them be of what station they may occupy Emperor or Princes must die. We are stationed on the hill out from Paw Paw Station and the ground is covered over with snow and I hope we may soon return home again to our quiet homes and have peace restored to our country again and all things right and our land may be as it once was[7]

---

[5] On March 1, 1862, the 110th Pennsylvania, along with other units in General Frederick Lander's division, moved toward Winchester. According to Ross Miller, a private in Company B, 110th Pennsylvania, Lander's troops departed from Paw Paw, Virginia (now West Virginia) around 5:00 p.m. Lander's command marched approximately seven miles and halted near Big Cacapon Creek. For further discussion see Bob Hileman, Jr., *The Crowther Letters: Family, Companions, and Rebels: Colonel James E. Crowther's Life Before and Military Experiences During the American Civil War* (Tarentum, PA: Hileman House, 2004), 185.

[6] On March 3, 1862, the *New York Times* wrote of Lander's death, "the fearless soldier, the bravest of the brave, [General Lander] died in camp at Pau Pau [*sic*], Western Virginia, from the effect of his wound received in the affair at Edward's Ferry. There is no officer in the army whose loss could cause a more profound and universal sorrow than that of Gen. LANDER." For further discussion of the circumstances surrounding General Lander's death on March 2, 1862, see Gary L. Ecelbarger, *Frederick W. Lander: The Great Natural American Soldier* (Baton Rouge: Louisiana State University Press, 2000), 277-279.

[7] A note on editorial style: Ephraim Burket never used periods to end an entry, as if to assure the diary he would be back to visit it again, so that has been maintained throughout. Additionally, the original spelling has been maintained.

March 3, Monday, 1862

Quite cold and frosty this morning but began to get quite mudy. The Regiments of this Division were all to appear on Parade at Paw Paw Station to pay their final adieu to the remains of Major Gen Lander of Massachusetts. There was about <u>18,000</u> on Parade. The remains were sent to his native state. We all expected to be in Winchester this evening but we was in Camp Tyler again. I don't know how long we may stay in this camp but I hope we may be successful.

March 8, Saturday, 1862

Cool this morning. The ground frozen some little and quite cloudy and Doctor Hays[8] gone to Cumberland and we got orders to draw and have three days rations on hand to go on the B&O R.R. to Martinsburg and be ready to march at any time. I packed up all the medicine and was ready to march at any time. There will be one company left behind to guard this place. I see 5 Locomotives now and all a heavy train to them loaded with wagons and soldiers and camping utensils. There was quite a number of soldiers going to Martinsburg our whole Division. There is quite a throng time on the Rail Road here today. Gen. [James] Shields has come to take command in Gen Landers deceased place. It looks pleasant out this evening

March 10, Monday, 1862

Quite cool this morning. We found ourselves the 110th Regt PV 40 miles down East of Paw Paw Station on the B&O R.R. We got out and built some fire and made coffee and was there all day. Some rain this morning and it rained several showers. It was very throng all day the car coming loaded with Government goods to Back Creek. This evening at 5 oclock the first train went over. I went over on it when the locomotives came on the bridge.[9] I gave some six inches on each side and it might have gone down

---

[8] Dr. David S. Hays, regimental surgeon. Hays mustered into service on December 4, 1861. Samuel P. Bates, *History of Pennsylvania Volunteers* (Harrisburg, PA: B. Singerly, State Printer, 1870), 3: 985.

[9] Other soldiers in this command wrote about this crossing, including William Brand, 66th Ohio Infantry. Brand described the scene of Union soldiers crossing the span: "The regiments of infantry, when leaving this morning, had to pass over a very narrow temporary suspension bridge spanning Back Creek at the railroad bridge from one abutment to the other without railing and about 75 feet high and as many long and only four feet wide... It was a pretty and interesting scene; the waving of the narrow bridge

in case it had gone some more or sliped off in the bottom. It was blown up last 4 July. We slept in the woods and quite cold all night. I don't often sleep in the woods at home this was Morgan Co. Va. Cleared off about 8 o'clock in evening

March 12, Wednesday, 1862

Quite pleasant this morning. We had nothing for breakfast accept [sic] a little coffee and one small sweet cracker.[10] The 3 Brigade the Ind 7 Ohio 7 & 29 & 110th Regt PV took up the line of march. Gen [Erastus] Tyler told us if we saw fit to follow him with out anything to eat as there was a chance for a fight again. Everyone gave three cheers and took up the line of march in our position in the Brigade. Came into within 4 miles of Winchester and halted for the night. We quartered in a field. We sleep out in the field. We are quartered where there was a fight or skirmish on. Yesterday routed the rebels and put them to flight and we marched 16 miles today without much to eat and I hope it was for a something. Our troops have possession of Winchester and the enemies have gone on towards Strasburg our army in pursuit

March 18, Tuesday, 1862

Quite a fine morning and the sun came up clear. At 3 oclock this morning we got orders to have three days rations in our haversacks and ready to march from Camp Shields. At 10 oclock pm we took up the line of march. The roads was fine and dry. We passed through Winchester and went on out on the Staunton and Winchester Turn Pike then came to Newtown 8 miles south of Winchester and passed through Middletown a small village. We passed through some fine country along the road and we heard in the afternoon some reports of cannon. We took up courage and marched on quite fast. We saw a grate smoke raise up and it was the Turnpike Bridge

---

and the stooping of the soldiers, with their heavily loaded knapsacks, passing under the timbers of the bridge now being erected– all in a single file while those behind were pressing their way forward; indeed it was as well worthy of a sketch from an artist as many others, already rendered famous by pen and pencil." See Daniel A. Master, ed., *Army Life According to Arbaw: Civil War Letters of William A. Brand 66th Ohio Volunteer Infantry* (Perrysburg, OH: Columbian Arsenal Press, 2019), 29. The bridge site is located ten miles west of Martinsburg, West Virginia.

[10] For further discussion of a soldier's diet see John D. Billings, *Hardtack and Coffee* (Boston: George M. Smith, Co., 1888), 108-142.

over Cedar Creek that the Confederates burnt that was the place where the fireing was done.[11] We marched on until dark we camped in a field without tents and had to sleep out of doors on the ground. The cavalry and 24 pieces of cannon and the caissons and the other fixings to cannon made 60 wagons and 6 horses in each waggon. It made a long string they passed us before we camped for the night. I was very much fatigued this evenning. The 3 Brigade was the advance collum [sic] the 2 & 1 Brigade following up. There was a grand sight to see the camp fires after night. We made coffee and eat our hard crackers. I ought not to have come along as I was unwell and very bad cold but I expected that we would have a fight soon or expecting to have one so I thought it best to go along for I did not like to stay back and I concluded to go I did go and hoping to see something

March 19, Wednesday, 1862

Quite cool this morning and somewhat cloudy. I found myself a soldier still this morning and in the 110th Regt Penn. Volunteers and in the 3rd Brigade our Brig Gen Tyler and under Gen Shields. We took up the line of march from where we was last night at 8 oclock this morning. Our Brigade in advance we crossed over Cedar Creek on a foot bridge that was built last night where the burnt bridge was only below near the water. The teams crossing below. We went on to within 1 mile from Strausburg then we was halted and skirmishers throwen out to see where the enemy was while we was resting the 24 pieces of cannon came past on the double quick. It looked like going to have a battle. The 6 cannon wagons passing the cavalry while we had haulted a while. We heard a report and they fired a shell it bursting in the air we cut off to the right through fields and the other Brigades went around to the left. We was haulted by Gen Tyler and loaded our guns and left the blankets overcoats and haversacks and the Gen Tyler said we was to support the artillary on the right and he wanted to know if we was going to do it. The response was that we would. Took up the line of march for about ¾ of a mile up towards the hills the artillery having placed their pieces and got the range and loaded our 3 Brigade to the right the artillary made a grand volley. Their troops soon got off they only made some 4 or 6 shots. It was a grand position for a battle our infantry in the rear of the cannon. There was some three of our

---

[11] For further discussion of this see Jonathan A. Noyalas, *Stonewall Jackson's 1862 Valley Campaign: War Comes to the Home Front* (Charleston, SC: History Press, 2010), 25.

cavalry horses killed by our shell as they advance beyond the place that they were to go to so our shell bursted and killed the three horses. There was none hurt accept one had his hand hurt slightly by a piece of shell. There was none of our men hurt. We went down to the Pike Bridge and went up the Pike with artillary and infantry and cavalry. We then came back to where our blankets were and over coats and haversacks and went up through a field and camped near the Turn Pike and made some coffee and making preparation for the night out in the open field without tents and it began to rain some and we got some orders to march again. The 3 Brigade took up the line of march down through Strausburg [sic] then to the left until they came to the Rail Road then down the Rail Road about one mile. They were doing some picket duty. They got into some sheds and shelter. Lieut [illegible possibly Kay or Ray] and I was in the ambulance and we stoped in town and hunted. We got into a house on the corner of Main Street on the left hand side. We had nothing but my shaul over us. I was on the sick list but we had to do the best we could for the night. It is hard to soldier when a person is not well. Our Gen Shields thought that we would have a hard fight out at Strausburg and they would not stand and our forces was too strong. There was a retreat of them. We came back. There was some talk that Jackson was reinforced and that he would make a stand and there was no stand but we must be subject to the laws of our Government and sustain them there and have a Constitution or we perish and may the stars and stripes wave[12]

March 21, Friday, 1862

It looks very much like winter this morning. I got up and I found the ground all covered with snow about one inch. This is the Equinoctial storm and I hope that we may have good weather. I looked down into the camp. There was not much stir as the soldiers are all very tired of their 22 mile march yesterday. Some of the men with scarcely any part of the soles of their shoes on and their feet very wett and there is no wonder that there so many sick or will be in a few days. I hope the war may soon be over and peace and prosperity may attend our country again[13]

---

[12] For an additional account of this movement south toward Strasburg see Hileman, Jr., *The Crowther Letters*, 201-203.

[13] Burket did not underestimate the toll the conflict had taken on the 110th Pennsylvania and other Union troops in Shields' division. On the day of this particular entry, March 21, 1862, one soldier in the 110th Pennsylvania Volunteer Infantry committed suicide as a result of exhaustion. Additionally,

We heard heavy cannonading yesterday afternoon out on the other side of Winchester. Our men had an engagement with the enemy. Our Artillary killed 62 men and several horses. There was one of our artillary men killed. Gen Shields got wounded in the arm by a piece of shell and broke his arm and the enemies fell back again. Our forces following in the evening at dusk[14]

March 23, Sunday, 1862

Quite cold this morning and damp and mudy. This morning we found our Regiment 110 PV along with 3 Brigade at Winchester at the north end of town. There all night without tents. We was ordered back to camp as we had no provision along. We got back at 10oclock and got our breakfast and got provision and at 2oclock the 3 Brigade took up the line of march towards Winchester and on out on the Strausburg Pike 4 miles. Our Battaries were fireing on the enemy all morning. We flanked off to the right about one ½ mile from the Pike then marched forward through the woods and at 20 minutes to 5oclock the 29 & 7 Ohio Regt 110th Regt P.V. 7th Indiana 1st Va. opened on the enemy with musketry at a furious rate and kept driving them back. They were behind a stone fence routing them made them retreat and followed them up until dusk when our men came back camped on the battlefield for the night. The doctors was buissy dressing the wounded men. We was running around until 12oclock at night. It was a hard fought battle our men taking several pieces of cannon and it was a hard looking battle field the dead the dying the wounded groaning with their cries yet many a brave man fell and killed and wounded. The number has not been ascertained yet but I think the enemy

---

only one in five soldiers in this command reported for duty. For further discussion see Kathryn Shively Meier, *Nature's Civil War: Common Soldiers and the Environment in 1862 Virginia* (Chapel Hill: University of North Carolina Press, 2013), 138.

[14] In the engagement on March 22, 1862, which occurred on Winchester's southern outskirts, General James Shields suffered a wound to his left arm when a shell fragment struck it. Shields also suffered a bruised shoulder and injured his left side. After Shields' wounding in the melee with Confederate troops commanded by Colonel Turner Ashby, field command of Shields' division fell upon the able shoulder of Colonel Nathan Kimball. For further discussion see Noyalas, *Stonewall Jackson's 1862 Valley Campaign*, 31.

killed 300 and wounded 150 men. Col Murray of the 84 Regt was killed in the engagement.[15] Capt [illegible possibly Gallagher] Co E 84 Regt killed 1st Lieut [note Burket left a long blank space in the journal here] 1st Lieut Linsey of the 14 Indiana Regt wounded 1st of the 14 wounded 1 Capt wounded 1 Lieut wounded of the 14 Indiana Lieut A Hopkins wounded Lieut Cogesberger wounded Lieut acting adjutant wounded Lieut acting adjutant wounded. The 110th Regt suffered [illeg.] heavy according to the number of men. We captured 235 prisnors and more taken on Sunday evening and we lost somewheres near a 100 men killed and 200 wounded. It was a very heavy fire and a very bold fight by both parties they made a heavy stand. The battle was supposed to have been one of the hardest fights that men generally get into. We lost a good many men and officers. I have saw men wounded in most all parts of their bodies head and the enemies were nearly all shot in the head that men killed on the old battleground. The trees have the bark all cut loose. I saw one man that had the whole top of his head blowen off by a shell.[16] The fight lasted 1 ¾ hours and was a hard fight and a desperate one and our men captured 2 cannon 4 caisons and the dead was being thick on the ground and the wounded also. The enemy here lost is supposed 300 killed 500 wounded and 237 prisnors. It is awful to think that we must have war among ourselves and so many families must suffer. Our loss in this fight is 100 killed 200 wounded and some have died of their wounds since the fight. There was 70 killed and 175 wounded of our forces[17]

---

[15] For additional information on Colonel William Murray see Roderick Rodgers Gainer, Jr., *Ultimate Sacrifice at the Battle of Kernstown: William Gray Murray, First Pennsylvania Colonel to Die in the American Civil War* (Shippensburg, PA: White Mane, 2007).

[16] This might be the same soldier David Hunter Strother described in his diary the following day. Cecil D. Eby, Jr., ed., *A Virginia Yankee in the Civil War: The Diaries of David Hunter Strother* (Chapel Hill: University of North Carolina Press, 1989), 19.

[17] Historian Gary L. Ecelbarger has treated the 110th Pennsylvania's conduct at the First Battle of Kernstown rather harshly. See Gary L. Ecelbarger, *"We Are In for It!": The First Battle of Kernstown* (Shippensburg, PA: White Mane, 1997), 136-137. For a counter to Ecelbarger's interpretation see Andy Waskie, "The 110th Pennsylvania Volunteers at Kernstown: The True Story," August 20, 2020, wesclark.com/jw/110thpa_at_kernstown.html. In the aftermath of the battle, according to Lieutenant Colonel James Crowther, the 110th Pennsylvania remained on the battlefield during the night of March 23 "without any fires and no supper and no breakfast next morning." For further

Quite cold this morning. I slept on the battlefield 4 miles South of Winchester and 1 ¼ West of the Pike. It was very cold all night I had not any breakfast or but one meal on Sunday I had a few pieces of hard crackers. We took up the line of march at 6 ½ oclock this morning for towards Strausburg. The cannonading commenced at 7oclock this morning the enemy falling back at 8 ½ oclock. Our cannon opened on them again on this side of the stone mills on the other side of [illeg. looks like Turnersville]. They soon began to fall back our forces following and on the other side 3 ½ miles of Newtown our cannon opened on them again. Our forces following up all the time reinforced by some 4 or 5 Regiments of Banks Division. There was some 3 or 4 Battaries came on our men was fighting them at Cedar Creek. There was some of the enemy killed today and wounded when we was 11 ½ miles from the town Winchester. Doct Hays got a dispatch to come back to Winchester to help to attend to the wounded so I had to come back get in this evening at 8oclock. I was nearly exhausted. When I got into that town I came to the Hospital the Union Hotel where I stayed all night. I slept on the floor all night. It was a fine day all day but we are of sadness too many more that have been wounded. The enemy retreated on over Cedar Creek and made a stand there and our Battaries soon made them get out of the way and some of the enemy was killed and their baggage train soon got off or they would have been captured our forces following up. The enemy had a grate manny killed. Our number not so many. We must expect something before long and I think down on the lower Potomac river and I hope we may soon return to our Quiet homes and be at peace. I hope and trust that I may live a life that I may die in peace

---

discussion of the regiment's involvement and condition in the aftermath of the First Battle of Kernstown see Hileman, Jr., *The Crowther Letters*, 206. The 110th Pennsylvania suffered seven enlisted men and four officers killed and thirty-nine wounded. Lieutenant William Kochersperger died from wounds received. U.S. War Department, comp., *War of the Rebellion: A Compilation of the Official Records of Union and Confederate Armies* (Washington, D.C.: U.S. Government Printing Office, 1880-1901), ser. 1, vol. 12, pt. 1, 346. After the war Union veterans who fought at the First Battle of Kernstown established the Winchester Club, an organization that met annually on the battle's anniversary to commemorate their victory over Stonewall Jackson with "a jolly, good time [of]... hard tack, coffee, stories, and fun." For further discussion see Noyalas, *Stonewall Jackson's 1862 Valley Campaign*, 48; *National Tribune*, March 26, 1885.

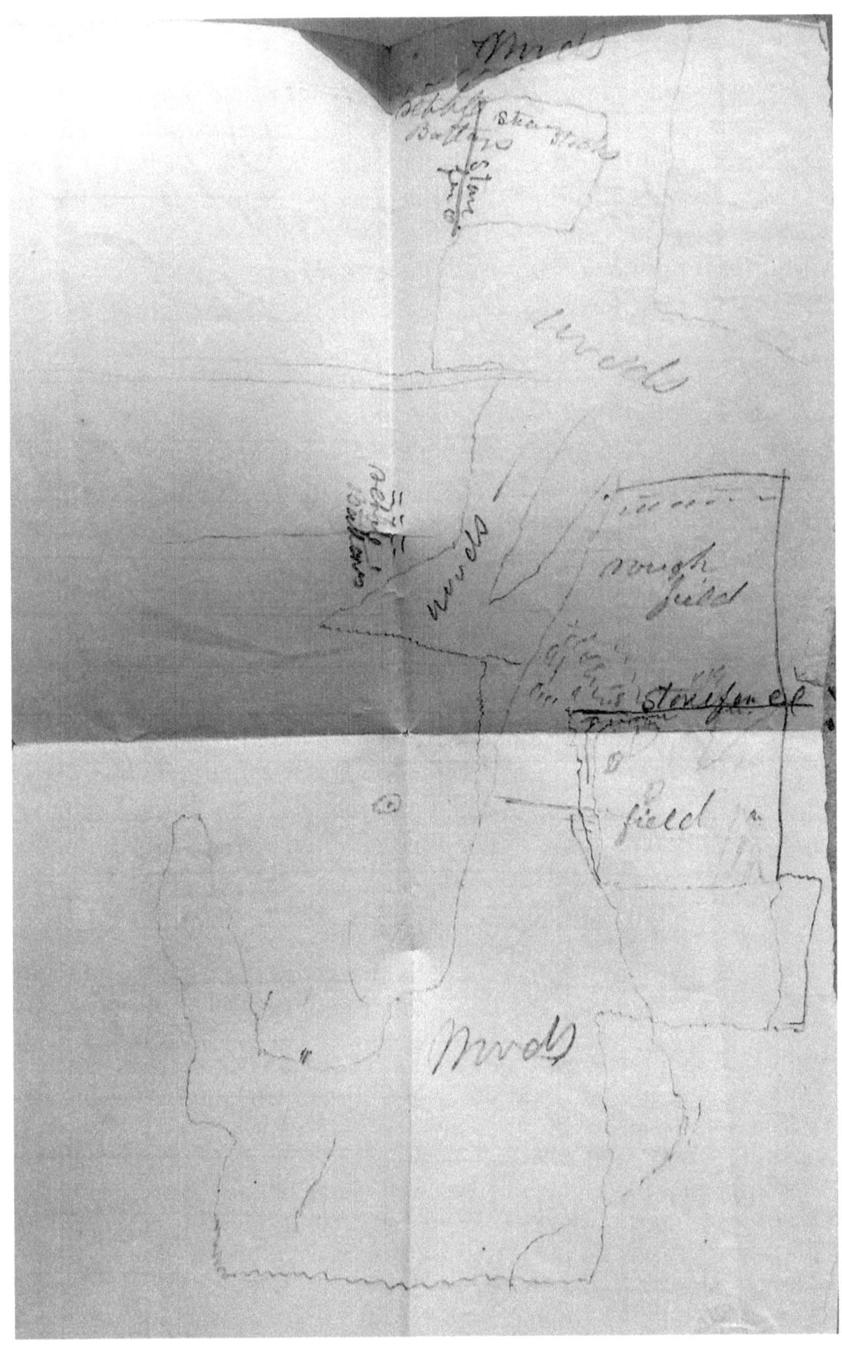

Burket's map of the First Battle of Kernstown
(*Courtesy Cheyenne Nimes*)

Quite cool this morning. I got up felt somewhat rested. I got up eat some few crackers for breakfast. I was helping to dress the wounded men. There was 4 amputations performed today 3 above the knee 1 below. It is hard for men to serve their country and then lose their limbs or arms and very very often their lives. There has been a fight out at Cedar Creek and driven back on the other side of Strausburg where they made a stand on the old battleground March 19 1862. They were soon rooted out of that place and fell back and losing their men and retreating all the time and I have not heard the result yet. I am now at the Union Hospital Winchester. The ladies are bringing in a grate many things for the wounded soldiers.[18] There was a CS Captain died last night and a Lieutenant of the CS. There was some 6 died last night. There are a good many that have died of their wounds. It is awful to think of these things. I have saw a grate deal and I hope I may live so I may always live and put my trust in him the allwise being and the giver of all things and believe in him the allwise giver oh I wish and pray that this war may soon come to a speedy close and peace be restored to our country and prosperity will or may attend us again. There was news came that there was a large lot of supplies coming on for the wounded soldiers and the sick. There a large lot of them. The poor wounded have to suffer much. I think the Doctors do not do their dutyor as much as they have a right to do and many a poor soldier die for the want of proper attention.[19] Oh I hope they will be attend in due time. They

---

[18] For additional discussion of the treatment of wounded after the battle and the role Winchester's women played in caring for both Union and Confederate wounded see Noyalas, *Stonewall Jackson's 1862 Valley Campaign*, 44-46.

[19] At the time of this entry the 110th Pennsylvania had one surgeon, Dr. David S. Hays, and one assistant surgeon, Dr. William Church. In the late spring of 1862 Surgeon Hays was chastised by Secretary of War Edwin Stanton for "shamefully" neglecting "a large detachment of sick and wounded men" sent to Washington, D.C. Appalled at Hays' conduct President Abraham Lincoln ordered Hays "dismissed from the service" for "gross dereliction of duty." Stephen Smith, M.D., ed., *The American Medical Times: Being a Weekly Series of the New York Journal of Medicine, January to July, 1862* (New York: Bailliere Brothers, 1862), 4: 352. Some, such as Henry Smith, surgeon general of Pennsylvania, came to Dr. Hays' defense. Smith penned in support of Hays: "After the battle at Winchester, March 23, 1862, I personally witnessed your untiring devotion to your duties in the Union Hotel hospital, and on my return to Pennsylvania I repeatedly spoke of them in terms of praise." *Report*

complain very much of having too much to do but what are they for. I do solemnly say they do not do as much as they are bound to do by their solemn vows and I hope the day may soon come that all such may be attended to and the needs relieve of their pains

March 26, Wednesday, 1862

Quite cool this morning the sun came up bright the sky clear. Found myself at the Union Hotel Hospital. I don't feel very well and I hope I may soon be well and live in peace and happiness at home with my family. There was 3 amputations performed today limbs taken off one above the knee two below the knee one was a confederate. It looks hard to see men have their limbs taken off. Our Regiment came back from Strausburg today. They look very tired and I hope they may have some rest and be able to refresh themselves up as we have saw service. There was two confederate officers died last night. They have gone to their long homes too. The ladies of this town of Winchester have been very kind today sending in refreshments and a grate many things that is nourishment to the wounded men. I have nothing new to put down this day. The men on the battlefield have all been buried and the trees looks as if there was a hard fought battle. It only lasted 1 ¾ hours and there was about 300 rebble killed 500 wounded of our men. Times are hard here[20]

March 27, Thursday, 1862

Quite cool this morning. I slept at the Union Hospital in Winchester. I came to the Regiment that was camped near the town to the right of the Pike to Strausburg and we have a very fine location and there is nothing new accept [sic] our forces are still routing <u>the</u> enemy and following them

---

of the Joint Committee on the Conduct of the War in Three Parts (Washington, D.C.: Government Printing Office, 1863), 507. On August 16, 1862, President Abraham Lincoln penned an endorsement on a letter from Pennsylvania governor Andrew G. Curtin asking "to revoke 'General Order No. 69. War Department,' dismissing" Hays. Lincoln noted that Hays "has previously enjoyed a good character as an efficient, energetic & kind hearted surgeon." See Roy P. Basler, ed., *The Collected Works of Abraham Lincoln* (New Brunswick, NJ: Rutgers University Press, 1953), 5: 380.

[20] For further discussion of the 110th Pennsylvania's activities in the days following the First Battle of Kernstown see Hileman, Jr., *The Crowther Letters*, 207-209.

up on the other side of Strausburg. They [the Confederates] have lost a grate many men and I don't see how they are going to do in regard to things.[21] The ladies are being kind to the wounded in Winchester and I hope that they may soon be well again and return to respective company. This is a very fine day

March 29, Saturday, 1862

I will try and look for better days and I hope that our land may be Union and peace and I trust that there will be no hard feeling in regard to this war after it is settled

March 30, Wednesday, 1862

Quite cool this morning but is somewhat like winter that is cold and it got somewhat pleasant. I found myself at Frederick Co. Winchester VA in the army of the United States in the 110th Regiment P.V. We had no lunch at this camp today and we have had but one Sermon since we left the state. Oh I am afraid some of our chaplins are rather careless and I think that some of them don't think much about the <u>future</u> wellfare of their fellow men.[22] I have been unwell for some time and I hope we may soon be where

---

[21] Two days after this entry Virginia's governor John Letcher, anticipating the Conscription Act going into effect throughout the Confederacy on April 16, 1862, ordered all militia units throughout the Commonwealth of Virginia disbanded and absorbed into existing Confederate regiments. For further discussion of this, the expansion of Jackson's ranks in the Valley, and the reaction of the Shenandoah Valley's Unionists, see Noyalas, *Stonewall Jackson's 1862 Valley Campaign*, 54-55.

[22] The chaplain of the 110th Pennsylvania Volunteer Infantry at the time was Jeremiah Schindel. Mustered into the regiment on December 28, 1861, Schindel was ordained a Luthern minister in 1831. In 1859 Schindel was elected to the Pennsylvania Senate representing Lehigh and Northampton Counties. He served as chaplain from December 28, 1861 until June 9, 1863. For discussion of the circumstances surrounding Schindel's court-martial in 1863 see Jeremiah Schindel, Court Martial Case File, April 1863, Court Martial Case Files, 12/1800-10/1894, RG 153, Records of the Office of the Judge Advocate General (Army) 1792-2010, NARA. After service with the 110th Pennsylvania, Schindel returned to his pastoral duties. He died in 1870. Bates, *History of Pennsylvania* Volunteers, 3: 985; *The Selinsgrove Times-Tribune*, July 13, 1870. For a succinct discussion of the role of regimental chaplains during the conflict see George C. Rable, *God's Almost Chosen Peoples: A Religious History of the American Civil War* (Chapel Hill: University of North Carolina Press, 2010), 112-114. For a more detailed examination see John W. Brinsfield, et. al., *Faith in*

the Sabbath day is respected and I hope the day may soon come

April 17, Thursday, 1862

It very fine this morning and is quite warm and the grain and clover and vegetation is putting fourth. I hope the time may soon come when all the nations may serve their god

April 22, Tuesday, 1862

Quite a cool morning. The wind was blowing some and still raising quite stormy all day. The <u>mud</u> is drying up some and nothing new that is of any importance. I hope that we will have pleasant weather. I was over at Masons House today. Things look as if there was soldiers about that did not care much[23]

May 5, Monday, 1862

Quite frosty this morning. We got orders this morning to pack up the medicines and be ready to move at 10 oclock. The Artillary and wagons was going all night. They were falling back to some other place or move on some other point. The road was crowded all day with Infantry Cavalry Artillary & Waggons for 20 hours. I never saw such a crowed. We was camped within 7 miles of Harrisonburg on the north side. We are now South 6 miles of New Market with Artillary on the Right and Left of the

---

the Fight: Civil War Chaplains (Mechanicsburg, PA: Stackpole Books, 2003), 3-96.

[23] Burket is referencing Selma, the home of Senator James Mason in Winchester. Mason's home was located at 514 Amherst Street. Selma, because Mason was the author of the controversial 1850 Fugitive Slave Law, was one of the earliest structures targeted by Union soldiers. Union troops began pulling the structure apart in the spring of 1862 and in late January 1863 Union general Robert H. Milroy, among the first to enforce President Abraham Lincoln's Emancipation Proclamation, razed what remained of the structure and utilized the material in the construction of fortifications north of Winchester. Garland R. Quarles, *The Story of One Hundred Old Homes in Winchester, Virginia* (Winchester, VA: Winchester-Frederick County Historical Society, 1967), 8-9; Cornelia McDonald, *A Diary with Reminiscences of the War and Refugee Life in the Shenandoah Valley, 1860-1865* (Nashville, TN: Cullom & Ghertner, 1935), 76, 132; Jonathan A. Noyalas, *"My Will is Absolute Law": A Biography of Union General Robert H. Milroy* (Jefferson, NC: McFarland, 2006), 87.

Pike. Our cannon have the Hills and their Battaries planted and our Brigade is to support the left. There are a grate many soldiers here. The 7 29 Ohio & 7 Indiana & 110th Penn V. are in the 3 Brigade. I heard today that Yorktown was taken. We came back 5 miles from where we had camped and we have fine camping ground. The roads was very dusty. I saw Gen Shields. He is a very plain man in his Dress & talk. He was with our Regiment awhile and told us that he could hold this position with 30,000 against 100,000 Soldiers. Our cannon can command the valley from one mountain to the other by occupying another hill... We left camp. Came on out on the road. 4 battaries passed us. Long train of wagons and the 4 & 8 Ohio Regts 14 Indiana Regt 7 & 13 Indiana 7 & 29 Ohio. I never saw such a train of wagons and soldiers as I have[24]

May 7, Wednesday, 1862

Frosty this morning and quite cold and the day is fine. We are in camp near the Battaries on the left. We have fine weather. I've received a letter from brother Jacob today. The report was that Richmond was taken by our forces and I hope that its true. We have been waiting for them to follow us up again so we may have a fight. No telling how soon we might have an attack. We was fixing up things some today. I repacked the medicines and have to cut our baggage down to a small bulk as we are expecting to have a long march somewhere I don't know where. But there is something in the wind we know what not. It looks for rain this evening some little but of no account and it is quite cool tonight

May 15, Thursday, 1862

Quite cloudy this morning. We packed our things on the waggons and got ready to march too up the line of march at 9½ oclock for the Gaines Cross Roads. We had good roads. It was not mudy until it rained some towards afternoon. The two Brigades come on and the Artillary also came some cavalry. I have not saw any good farms today. We came out 10 miles today. We camped near a mill. It was quite wet this evening and will be very disagreeable to camp out. We got a mail this morning. I received two letters this morning and one paper. It is raining quite fast this evening. We

---

[24] On this date, Jackson Hicks, a laborer before the conflict, deserted from the regiment. Six days later Sergeant Thomas Bentley deserted from the regiment. Descriptive List of Deserters, Pennsylvania State University, July 30, 2020, digital.libraries.psu.edu/digital/collections/digitalbks2/id/90735.

*are in among the hills and mountains and rather broken land. We have
water handy and camped on side of the hill– or fort rather... Today the
Magor of the 1ˢᵗ Va. who is Magor Chamberlin who was making ~~a charge~~
something of advance.*[25] *He was cut off by 11 Rebel cavalry. He drew his
sword and held it out until [illegible Hes or Lees?] came near them and
he put spurs to his horse and made a dash through them. They fired on
him but did come off Victorious. Our cavalry had a small skirmish with
the enemy today near Flint Town. It is said that this cavalry is Stewarts
cavalry. Bully for him*

May 23, Friday, 1862

*Quite cool this morning and all appearance for a fine warm day away
down in Va. Stafford Co. I was all night with John Patterson 5 PV
Reserve.*[26] *We went down to the 7 Regt P.V.R. to see Mr Kinsgan.*[27] *He had
gone to Washington. He was sick. We came back to the 5 and then came
up to where our Regt & Brigade was camped. We have a good view of
Fredericksburg Va. The day was awful warm. President A Lincoln was
here viewing Gen McDowalls Troops. I saw him. He is plain in his dress
and there was quite a crowed out to see him.*[28] *I received 4 Letters and 14
Papers. Nothing new of importance that I know of and I hope we will soon
get home*

---

[25] The "Chamberlin" to whom Burket refers is Major Benjamin F.
Chamberlain, 1ˢᵗ West Virginia Cavalry (referred to as 1ˢᵗ Regiment of Loyal
Virginia Volunteer Cavalry until West Virginia's establishment in 1863).
Chamberlain was commissioned major on November 11, 1861. He resigned his
commission in October 1863. For further discussion see Theodore F. Lang,
Loyal West Virginia From 1861-1865 (Baltimore, MD: The Deutsch Publishing
Co., 1895), 159. The event Burket references is briefly discussed in C.J. Rawling,
History of the First Regiment Virginia Infantry (Philadelphia: J.B. Lippincott,
1887), 78.

[26] A reference to Sergeant John J. Patterson who mustered into the 5ᵗʰ
Pennsylvania Reserves on June 21, 1861. Patterson transferred to the Veteran
Reserve Corps in 1863. Bates, *History of Pennsylvania Volunteers*, 1: 688.

[27] No one with this surname appears on the roster of the 7ᵗʰ Pennsylvania
Reserves. Burket may be referring to Philip Klinger, a musician in the
regiment. Klinger enlisted on May 4, 1861. Bates, *History of Pennsylvania
Volunteers*, 1: 737.

[28] Earl Schenck Miers, ed., *Lincoln Day by Day: Chronology, 1809-1865*
(Washington: Lincoln Sesquicentennial Commission, 1960), 3: 114.

Quite cool and a very heavy dew this morning. We found our 4 Brigade on the Road all night. Marched some 3 or 4 miles but did not march much until after 12.0.clock. We passed over some very rough roads last night. The 1ˢᵗ 2 & 3 Brigades marched all night on towards Frount [sic] royal. We haulted after the sun was up and had some breakfast. Which we relished very much although it only consisted of coffee hard crackers and meat... We haulted 1 ½ hour after we marched a short distance and we then took up the line of march. We came along near the market manasses gap Rail Road. We passed Linden Station and we came on to Frount [sic] royal where we arrived at 6.oclock this evenning. The C.S. Army had left to day some time the where house we have there was a lot of WS Government stores was set on fire by the C. Army. The house was burnt down. There was 3 or 4 cars burnt and among them was 1,360 stand of Harpers Ferry muskets burnt and tents and some 3 or 400 bussheled corn. Our men rather took them by surprise that is Gen Shields Division. The New Hampshire cavalry made a charge on one Regt of the C.A. and our men took some prisners 135 in all 2 cassions that was left in town some sabers. The Capt Ainsworth Capt of N. Hampshire cavalry was killed and 7 privates.²⁹ There was some of the Confederates killed but is not knowen how many. Some of our men were wounded. Our men recaptured Col. Kinly mager of the NH cavalry and 1 agdugant [sic] and some 13 others.³⁰ It rained quite a shower this afternoon about 3.oclock and this evening we camped near the town the Edge of it. I was up town I saw the prisners. I hope I long that we may soon have this war settled in some way or other as it is a grate destruction to the Life and Property on both sides. The baggage train of the 4 Brigade did not get in to camp they were some 5 miles from this place. We have marched 280 miles since the 29 of April

---

[29] This is a reference to Captain William Ainsworth, a native of New Hampshire, who served in the 1ˢᵗ Rhode Island Cavalry. Ainsworth was killed in this fight, struck by eight Confederate bullets. For further discussion of the circumstances surrounding Ainsworth's death see Rev. Frederic Denison, *Sabres and Spurs: The First Regiment Rhode Island Cavalry in the Civil War, 1861-1865* (Central Falls, RI: E.L. Freeman & Co., 1876), 89. For discussion of the circumstances of that fight see Peter Cozzens, *Shenandoah 1862: Stonewall Jackson's Valley Campaign* (Baton Rouge: Louisiana State University Press, 2008), 404-406.

[30] Rev. Frederick Denison, regimental historian of the 1ˢᵗ Rhode Island Cavalry, noted that the unit captured 117 Confederates and seized twenty Union prisoners taken by Confederates. See Denison, *Sabres and Spurs*, 89.

last. We have done some very hard marching within the last mounth and we feel the affects of it. The men have very sore feet

June 4, Wednesday, 1862

Raining this morning and we have roused up quite early.[31] At 5oclock we took up the line of march from near Lieurey [Luray] to Columbian bridge. It rained very hard all day. The men have been doing that which is wrong in the sight of God and many have been stealling braking into stores shops along the road side. I feel for the women and children and old age men who can't work. I dislike the way they in many instances taking that which is not their own especially from citizens.[32] The roads are very bad we marched 12 miles today. Camped in the woods on the left of the road. It rained on until 5oclock when I quite heard cannon some wheres I know not. I will close. The ground is very soft and the river high and all streams

June 8, Sunday, 1862

Quite a fine morning. The sun came up bright and I find myself a soldier in the U.S. army and away down in the State of Virginia Page Co. There is no Sabbath day here in the army and very little Preaching. We were roused up last night at 12 oclock to march on as our advance was <u>marching</u> on that is the cavalry and we had to follow up which was 10 miles to Port Republic. We marched on. The 4 Brigade 7 Indiana 1st Va 84 & 110 Penn V.I. now the only forces that was along with 4 pieces of brass cannon and a small squad of cavalry. Our Brig Gen Carroll went into the town this morning. Made a dash cleard the bridge and soon crossed the bridge planted 2 cannon on the East side and they had a good possition and we had not and we had no rifle cannon here at that time. Only think of Gen Carroll attacking about 20000 of the enemy with about 1000 men in all of ours. They had some 30 cannon and long range ones. Our men keep up the fire for sometime. They captured the 2 brass cannon that was on the west side. There was a good many killed out of the 7 Ind Regt. There was some 6 or 8 horses killed and 2 Artillary men killed. This fireing took place about 8oclock in the morning. We were reinforced by Gen Tyler in the

---

[31] For additional discussion of rainfall at this time see Robert K. Krick, *Civil War Weather in Virginia* (Tuscaloosa: University of Alabama Press, 2007), 55-62.

[32] Burket was not the only one appalled by Union soldiers making war against the civilian population in the Shenandoah Valley. For additional discussion see Noyalas, *"My Will is Absolute Law,"* 50-51.

afternoon by some 2000 men Infantry. We had to fall back some distance 2 miles when Tylers Brigade came up. We fell back on the ground the only place where we could make a stand. We also was reinforced by one Battary of 6 Parrot cannon long range a Regular Battary. Biovouacked for the night on the ground that we intend making a stand[33]

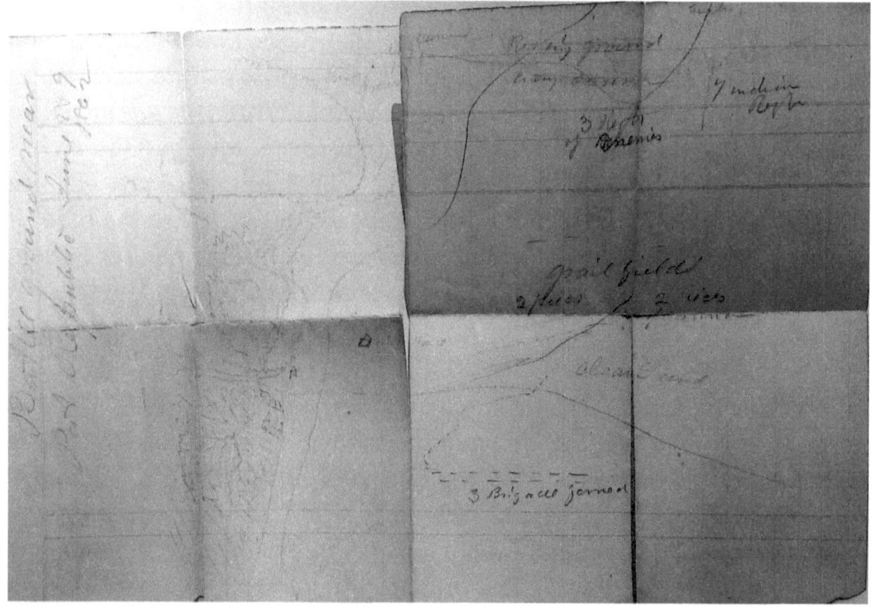

Burket's sketch of Port Republic
(*Courtesy Cheyenne Nimes*)

June 9, Monday, 1862

Quite a bright morning. The sun came up quite bright. I sleept very sound last night although we were in a bad position. Our men had a strong picket out last night. All things quiet last night. Early this morning the enemy commenced fireing on our men the cavalry. Our cannon soon opened with a shell noise with the yelling bomb shell whistling and them burst. The 84 & 110th Regt were supporting the Left of the Battaries. They filled up into the woods which was a hill. There was [note: in pencil, "three" is written

---

[33] For the best analysis of the Battle of Cross Keys, June 8, 1862, see Robert K. Krick, *Conquering the Valley: Stonewall Jackson at Port Republic* (Baton Rouge: Louisiana State University Press, 1996), 137-275.

over "two"] three of our cannon at the foot of the hill on a coal hearth and the rest were down in the grain fields. The 7 Indiana Regt Col Gavin commander fought 3 Regt of the enemy. They keept their ground for about one hour when they advanced. They made them retreat and fired on them all the way [note: word "Battle" at top]. The 7 Indiana Regt. retreated but in good order. They kept fireing all the way on their retreat. The enemy took Part of Capt Clarksons Battary and our men retook them again. Our Cannoneers made desperate [illegible havoc?] amoung the enemy with Grape and canister. Some of the cannoneers fired 40 rounds of grape and canister. The enemy came on our left Flank before our men saw them as the woods came to the road that goes to Port Republic as the fight took place within 1 ½ mile of the village. We lost a good many men. Some 250 to 300 wounded and 200 or 250 killed and some 500 missing. The enemy lost a grate many killed and wounded. Our men fought desperately like tigers but they were overpowered and our men to make a retreat fast. It was done In fine order. The 3 Brigade was in the Battle to day which consisted of the 5...29... [note: "62" crossed out] 66...7 Ohio Regiments were in the Battle. The 4 Brigade consisted the 1st Va. 7 Ind. & 84 & 110th Regt. [Pennsylvania] There was only some 3000 of our men in the Battle. I saw many wounded soldiers some fatally some that would soon try the realities. [note: letter "y" in "realitys" crossed out]. We fell back 15 miles and there camped for the night. It was wet the ground very full of water. Although we had to do the best we could we are all very much woren out and need rest very bad. The wounded were all brot back to Lieurey [Luray] in the Ambulances. Some of the wounded suffered very much. We lost our Medicine box to day and there was a grate many things lost. There was 7 pieces of our cannon captured by the Enemy. We took one of their Parrot cannon. There was 9 of our cannon taken and 6 caissons. We lost a good many muskets. The 7 Indiana Regiment lost 180 in all and the 110th took about 125 men into the fight and lost some 40 in all killed wounded and taken Prisners. Towards evenning Gen Freemont attacked them and routing them capturing a grater part of their cannon. The enemy burnt the most of their baggage train before Freemont could capture it and I don't know if he captured any of their men or not. The shells came very close to me today. The destruction of Life was grate[34]

---

[34] For the finest examination of the Battle of Port Republic see Krick, *Conquering the Valley*, 277-455.

June 11, Wednesday, 1862

Quite cool this morning and we had some breakfast and got marching orders and we soon was ready to take up the line of march and we all came back to Lieurey [Luray]. Came on out 2 miles from Town. The road was very mudy. I have been very much woren out and we came through Lieurey. We saw a grate many wounded soldiers looking out of the windows. We have good camping now. There was some shell came in today that was missing. There was a lot of soldier that was taken Prisners at Port Republic out of the 1st Va Regiment.[35] They broke out of the gaurdhouse and made their escape. I don't see how any of us escaped that we was not all taken Prisners in the Battle as they had some 20,000 of a force against us. We have marched since the 29 of April up to this evening 403 miles and since the 12 of May 343 miles marching nearly every day through rain mud up to our knees wadeing creeks up to our waists and then lay down at night on the wet ground without blankets or tents. I have not sleept in a bed since the 1st of February last. I have saw the hardships of a soldiers life many times not as much as we could eat but had to do the best we could we are among the hills and pspurs [illeg. maybe aspens] of the Blue ridge and we have traveled over some awful roads since we have been on this march. I am now give out. I have the Rheumatism and I will soon have to give up as I am entirely woren out and can't get along much longer. I must soon do something as I have stood it longer than if I had been at home

June 12, Thursday, 1862

Quite cool this morning. It was quite cool last night. We have camped Two miles East of the Town of Luerey [Luray] Page Co. Va. There was about 100 waggons took wounded and sick back to Frount [sic] royal to day to be sent to Washington City. The day was very warm. I don't feel very well as I am woren out and weak that I can't stand much more. I have the Rheumatism and pain in the back. I got a Furlough to go home for thirty days to [illegible secure?] my health as I must do something or I will be no use.[36] We have about 180 wounded men that were sent to Frount

---

[35] For additional discussion of the role the 1st Virginia played in the fight see Rawling, *History of the First Regiment*, 94-97.

[36] For further discussion of the practice of granting medical furloughs see Adams, *Doctors in Blue*, 157. Ailments and illness plagued soldiers on both sides during this time. For a broader discussion in the Union army during 1862 see Stephen Sears, *To the Gates of Richmond: The Peninsula Campaign* (New

[sic]Royal that were wounded in the Battle on Monday

June 14, Saturday, 1862

I did not sleep very well last night as we had no covering and a hard floor to sleep on. We got up in the morning as the sun came up bright. I made some coffee and we eat some dry hard crackers and had to be satisfied as we are in the land where we can't expect anything good to eat as we are Among the schells. The wounded and sick are all being put in the cars. They are freight cars. There are 304 in all and a lot of prisners 135 in the same train. We got started from Frount [sic] Royal Warren Co. Va. at 11½ oclock. P.M. There was a good many had to get on the top of the cars I was on the top. The sun was very warm and the smoke from the Engine made it very unpleasant although we had a good view of the surrounding country the Manasses gap through the mountains. We passed near where the Bull Run ~~fight~~ Battleground. I saw where the rebels had thrown up Breast works and had a lot of cabins built for winter quarters. There is a very bad stench there. The country looks quite level towards Cattells Station. The Bull run Battleground is roleing and I think the part I saw would not stope the famous Gen Shields Division in case he had men. They must leave their strong holds and flee to other parts of the Country. Over the country is very poor along this Rail Road. There is a grate deal of land woren out and is now a forest again. The land has been worked out by neglect and for the want of energy ambition but they have found the raising of Negroes more profitable and selling them to the more extreme Southern States and leaving their tilling of the land to Overseers and Negroes for the Productions. We arrived at the Town of Alexandria below Washington City at sun down and at 8 ½ oclock we arrived in the Town of Washington City. D.C. We came to the Soldiers Retreat and went to bed without supper lay on the floor. We were very much fatigued. I feel bad this evening somewhat sick. This is the first time I have been in this city the Seat of our Government where all the archives of the nations is recorded and our Ruler or President resides. The time has come when the South needs a new race of people to cultivate the land and destroy the Selling of Humane Flesh from one state to another or person and I hope the Southern schivelry [sic] will soon be wiped out of Existence and men of pure motives settle the land where they can live in peace with their fellow men and may peace soon be restored to our land

---

York: Ticknor & Fields, 1992), 347-348.

Although regimental records indicate that Burket received a promotion to second lieutenant in Company D on July 12, 1862, and then on August 9, 1862, received a promotion to captain in the same company, evidence indicates that he never returned to the 110th Pennsylvania after his thirty-day furlough expired in July. Burket made the final entry in his diary on July 5, 1862. In it he noted that he attended a picnic and that a Lutheran minister drove him home in a "spring waggon."[37] Burket officially resigned his commission on December 20, 1862.[38] Burket died on January 17, 1901, at his farm in Sinking Valley. His obituary noted that "illness" and "general debility" plagued him in the final year of his life. Regarded "as a good citizen, with a large circle of relatives and friends," Burket was buried in Saint John's Lutheran Cemetery in Blair County, where his service in the 110th Pennsylvania is forever marked by the simple inscription on his tombstone "Co. D 110 Regt. P.V." and the five-pointed star of the Grand Army of the Republic.[39]

Ephraim Burket's tombstone
(*Photo by Michelle Pedersen*)

---

[37] In his diary entry for July 5, 1862, Burket notes it was "Rev. Crist" who "brot us over in the spring wagon."
[38] Details about Burket's promotions and resignation can be found in Bates, *History of Pennsylvania Volunteers*, 3: 994.
[39] *Altoona Tribune*, January 18, 1901.

"Our Guns Belched Forth Their Thunder"
Battery G, First Rhode Island Light Artillery in the Shenandoah
Valley, Autumn 1864

Robert Grandchamp

Throughout August 1864 General Philip H. Sheridan bided his time collecting men and supplies at Harpers Ferry. Throughout the month, Sheridan's command maneuvered between Harpers Ferry and Fisher's Hill in what one Union soldier termed a "mimic war."[1] Sheridan understood that if he was too zealous it might cost Lincoln the upcoming election. Sheridan understood that much rode on his decisions in the Valley. "I deemed it necessary to be very cautious... the fact that the Presidential election was impending made me doubly so, the authorities at Washington having impressed upon me that the defeat of my army might be followed by the overthrow of the party in power," Sheridan explained.[2] The "mimic war," which defined Sheridan's first month in command ended on September 19. Around 2:00 a.m. on September 19 Sheridan's Army of the Shenandoah marched toward Winchester along the Berryville Pike, where elements of Confederate general Jubal Early's army waited near the banks of Opequon Creek. The cavalry had been engaged since early morning as General Horatio Wright hurried the Sixth Corps along. The second and third divisions were thrown into the fight around 11:30 a.m. The first division was initially held in reserve as the other two attacked. Waiting patiently to open fire on the Confederate line were the cannoneers of Battery G, First Rhode Island Light Artillery.[3]

---

[1] Jeffry D. Wert, *From Winchester to Cedar Creek: The Shenandoah Campaign of 1864* (Mechanicsburg, PA: Stackpole Books, 1997), 29-45.
[2] Philip H. Sheridan, *Personal Memoirs of P.H. Sheridan* (New York: Charles L. Webster & Co., 1888), I: 499-500.
[3] Wesley Merritt, "Sheridan in the Shenandoah Valley" in *Battles and Leaders*

Although not initially engaged, the troops held in reserve faced a horrific barrage of bullets and artillery shells. The Confederate artillery fired sporadically at the Union line. As he waited with Battery G to go in, Corporal James A. Barber remembered, "The fire from the Rebel Batteries became very annoying." The infantry kept looking over their shoulders, waiting for support. Wright knew that it was too early in the engagement to send in the first division so he ordered Colonel Charles Tompkins, commanding the Sixth Corps Artillery brigade, to deploy several batteries into the fray at 2:30 p.m. That morning Sheridan informed Tompkins he wanted to "see some dead horses before night." In other terms, he was to sacrifice his batteries if necessary to win the battle.[4]

Tompkins saw a point of advantage on the right of the Sixth Corps' line and sent in the Fifth Maine Battery and First New York Battery on the right, or north side, of the Berryville Pike. The colonel then returned to his column and sent in Battery G and the First Massachusetts Battery. Captain George W. Adams, Battery G's charismatic commander, obeyed as the battery dashed into an open field on the left, or south side, of the Berryville Pike. Promptly unlimbering, the Rhode Islanders kept up a galling fire of shell and canister, depending on the target, engaging the Confederates near Winchester. The artillery fire proved a morale booster for Sheridan's infantry. Lieutenant Colonel Aldace Walker of the Vermont Brigade wrote, "The batteries were nearer the front that day than we had ever seen before." Through the tremendous smoke to their front, General William R. Cox's brigade of North Carolinians started to approach the two batteries, intent on capturing them. Seeing the threat, Captain William H. McCartney, commanding the First Massachusetts, ordered his men to prepare to limber up and retire to escape the threat. Adams' Battery was going nowhere, and the Bay Staters blocked the Rhode Islanders from engaging the enemy.[5]

<hr>

of the Civil War (Edison, NJ: Castle, 1956), 4: 503-510.

[4] John F. L. Hartwell, Ann H. Britton, and Thomas J. Reed, *To My Beloved Wife and Boy at Home: The Letters and Diaries of Orderly Sergeant John F.L. Hartwell* (Madison, NJ: Fairleigh Dickinson University Press, 1997), 286-290; Aldace F. Walker, *The Vermont Brigade in the Shenandoah Valley: 1864.* (Burlington, VT: Free Press Association, 1869), 103-104.

[5] U.S. War Department, comp., *War of the Rebellion: A Compilation of the Official*

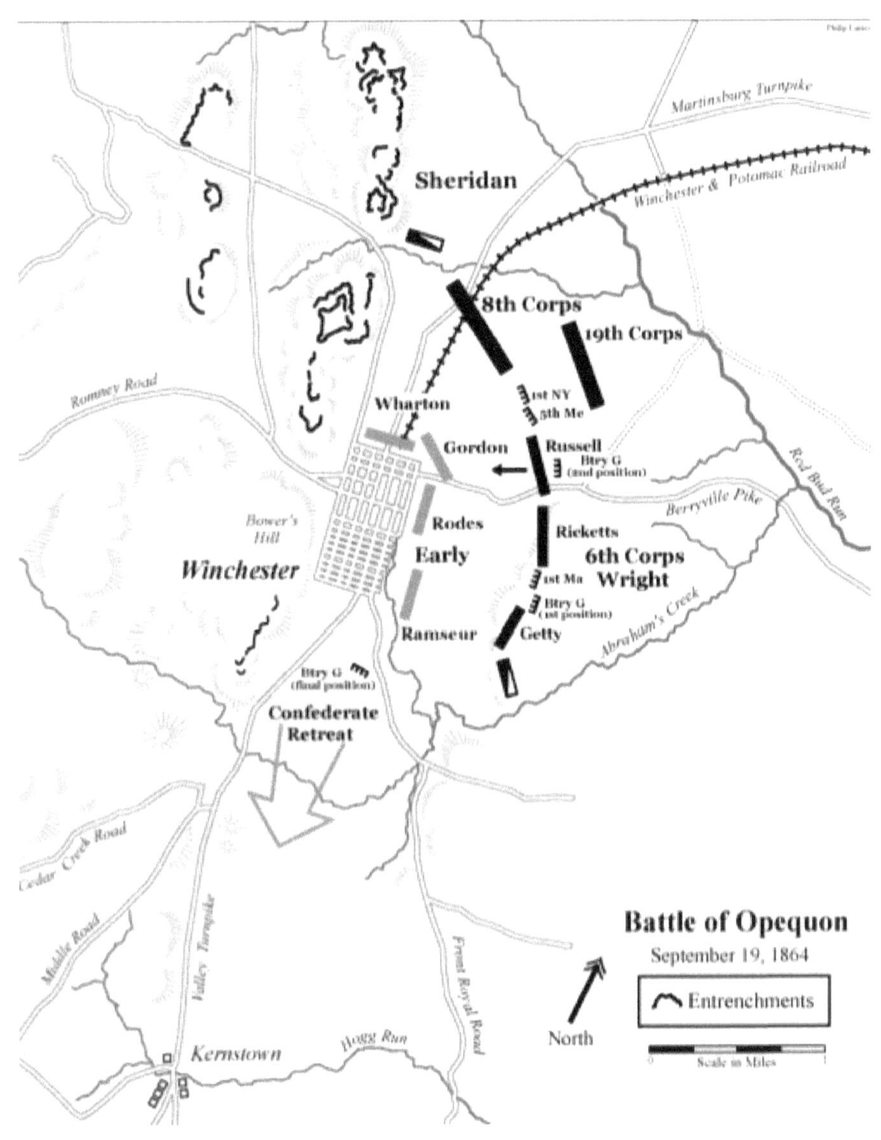

Map of the Third Battle of Winchester
(*Courtesy Robert Grandchamp*)

Records of the Union and Confederate Armies (Washington, D.C.: U.S. Government Printing Office, 1880-1901), ser. I, vol. 43, 149-153, 271-272. (hereafter cited as *O.R.*) Walker, *Vermont Brigade*, 103-104. Frank M. Flinn, *Campaigning with Banks in Louisiana, '63 and '64 and with Sheridan in the Shenandoah Valley in '64 and '65.* (Boston: W.B. Clarke, 1889), 183-185.

In the confusion of the battle, Captain McCartney regained his composure and redeployed the First Massachusetts. To his left, Captain George Adams knew what was coming. He calmly barked out the command for canister as the number seven men pulled the round out of the chests, passed it to the number five, who then ran it to number two. The four Rhode Island guns waited for the opportune moment to engage. At four hundred yards, Adams gave the command to open fire as the Rhode Islanders and Bay Staters blasted the deadly rounds as the North Carolinians moved closer. Adams made the crucial command decision to stay in position, even at the risk of losing the guns. The decision to remain proved the right one as Battery G's fire "checked the enemy." [6] Corporal James Barber noted that "We opened such a murderous fire on the Rebels that the battery soon drove them from their position."[7] Private Thomas J. Watkins, a veteran in Cox's command, wrote of the effectiveness of Adams' cannon: "We ran against a rock fense in a piece of woods defended by a yankee line and a masked battery. That opened on us. There General R. E. Rodes was killed by a piece of shell. The most of the guns of this battery were loaded with grape and canister doing some damage to our unprotected lines; the writer found a large oak stump that was sound and he took position behind this making as safe a protection as our[s] would need."[8]

Following the repulse of Cox's attack, Colonel Tompkins galloped up from the right of the line and redeployed Battery G onto the right, or north side, of the Berryville Pike, now eight hundred yards from the enemy as shell and case shot became the primary weapons of choice. Again, with the First Massachusetts Battery, the two commands worked in tandem to destroy the Virginia Amherst Artillery that attempted to enfilade Wright's second division. By this time in the war, the Confederate artillery had become not much of a factor on the battlefield: low on ammunition, horses, and guns. Still it presented a nuisance as Sheridan prepared to deliver the

---

[6] *O.R.* ser. I., vol. 43, 149-153: 271-272. John Russell Bartlett, *Memoirs of Rhode Island Officers, Who Were Engaged in the Service of Their Country During the Great Rebellion of the South: Illustrated with Thirty-Four Portraits.* (Providence: Sydney S. Rider, 1867), 380.
[7] James A. Barber Diary, September 19, 1864, John Hay Library, Brown University, Providence, RI (items from this repository hereafter cited as JHL).
[8] Thomas J. Watkins, "Reminiscences," courtesy of Scott C. Patchan.

final blow. The fire became very effective as the Rhode Islanders sighted the guns with precision. The results were seen immediately.[9]

Henry Berkeley, one of the members of the Amherst Battery, wrote about the destruction the gunners from Massachusetts and Rhode Island inflicted on his command: "At one time came a Yankee shell which struck the middle horse of my limber right between the eyes, and bursting took off the middle horses head, cut off the hind legs of the saddle horse in front of him and the front legs of the horse behind him, cut out the pole of the limber in two places, and passed through the limber box, which fortunately was nearly empty." Two limbers were blown up, in addition to killing the eight horses that pulled them and some of the drivers. These were just a few of the 462 rounds fired this day.[10]

In the battle's aftermath Union soldiers who walked the battlefield seemed sickened by the destruction wrought by the Union artillery. Private Frank M. Flinn, 38th Massachusetts Infantry, wrote, "The dead were horrible dead. It seemed as if the majority had received their death from shells. Most of the bodies were mangled beyond recognition. Our artillery, borne across the plateau to its farthest verge, did a work so terrible, that to witness it was sickening." The artillery accomplished the vital task of holding the Confederates back, while the corps commanders made final preparations for the counterassault.[11]

Around 3:00 p.m. Wright's first division commanded by General David Russell entered the fray. General Wright recorded of the scene: "The First Division moved admirably on the enemy, and the batteries with canister opened upon them with murderous effect, the two driving them back in much disorder. This was the turning point in the conflict." General Robert Rodes, a Confederate division commander tried to push his men forward when he was struck down by a shell fragment from a Sixth Corps gun. The movement of Russell's division was followed by simultaneous blows from the rest of the Sixth Corps, in addition to the Eighth and Nineteenth. Pressure from Sheridan's three infantry corps, coupled

---

[9] *O.R.* ser. I, vol. 43, 149-153, 271-272. Barber, Diary, September 19, 1864, JHL.
[10] Paul Mathless, ed. *Shenandoah 1864* (Richmond, VA: Time Life Books, 1998), 94.
[11] Flinn, *Campaigning*, 188-191.

with the crushing blow delivered by Sheridan's cavalry to that portion of the Confederate line which faced north that afternoon, crumbled Early's line. As Early's line collapsed and his command retreated south toward Fisher's Hill, Early placed artillery in an attempt to cover the retreat, but that effort proved futile as the First Massachusetts and Rhode Island Batteries C and G, forced the Confederate gunners to retreat.

The Third Battle of Winchester, what Union soldiers referred to as the Battle of Opequon, proved a decisive Union victory. After the battle, one which resulted in approximately 9,000 combined casualties, 5,000 Union and 4,000 Confederate, General Wright praised his artillerists, including Colonel Tompkins and Captain Adams, for the important role they played. Wright wrote, "The artillery of this corps alone expended eighteen army wagon-loads of ammunition, and all with good effect upon the results of the conflict. All of my batteries were effectively engaged." In the battle's aftermath Battery G helped to guard 500 captured prisoners.[12]

With Winchester firmly secured, Sheridan had an invasion point and supply base to launch attacks further south, up the Valley. On September 20 Sheridan's Army of the Shenandoah marched south. By late afternoon that day Sheridan's army approached the environs of Strasburg and spied Early's command positioned atop Fisher's Hill—the narrowest point in the Valley and the last place Early believed he could make a defensive stand before abandoning the northern Shenandoah Valley.[13] Two days later the Army of the Shenandoah struck Early's army.[14]

Anchored on its western flank by Little North Mountain and Massanutten Mountain on its eastern end, Tumbling Run traversing the ground in its front, and strengthened with earthworks, Fisher's Hill possessed all of the hallmarks of a strong defensive position. However, Fisher's Hill's benefits could be realized only if Early's command possessed enough troops to

---

[12] *O.R.* ser. I, vol. 43, 149-153: 271-272. Barber, Diary, September 19, 1864, JHL.

[13] For additional discussion of Early's decision to make a defensive stand at Fisher's Hill see Jonathan A. Noyalas, *The Battle of Fisher's Hill: Breaking the Shenandoah Valley's Gibraltar* (Charleston, SC: History Press, 2013), 21-24.

[14] Barber Diary, September 20-22, 1864, JHL; Merritt, "Sheridan in the Shenandoah," 510-513.

adequately defend the 3.9-mile span from mountain to mountain. Unfortunately for Early he did not. Captain Samuel Buck of the 13th Virginia noted simply that "the position was a very strong one, but our army was too small to man it."[15]

Around 4:00 p.m. General George Crook's Eighth Corps launched the assault against Early's weakly protected left flank. Once Crook's command struck Early's western flank defended by the poorly equipped troopers from General Lunsford Lomax's command and General Stephen D. Ramseur's division, the Union Sixth and Nineteenth Corps readied themselves for the assault. As troops from General George Getty's division moved forward to attack that portion of Early's line defended by the Confederate division commanded by General John Pegram, Confederate cannon, more than likely from Colonel Carter M. Braxton's artillery battalion, opened fire.[16] To counter what brigade commander General Daniel Bidwell characterized as "heavy artillery fire" from Braxton's guns, Colonel Tompkins received orders to open fire. The twenty guns, including Battery G unlimbered and soon began "pouring shot and shell into their works with marvelous rapidity and accuracy."[17]

Battery G's old companions, the Vermont Brigade, supported Tompkins' guns. A few Confederate shells landed in the ranks, but not enough apparently to cause any significant alarm. As the Union assault gained momentum and the Confederate line collapsed like dominoes falling from west to east, the only element of Early's command that maintained any modicum of composure was his command's artillery as they fired at their attackers. Still they proved no match for Tompkins' cannon. Wilbur Fisk, a soldier in the Second Vermont recalled the accuracy of the Sixth Corps' cannon: "The artillery fired with remarkable precision. Although the Rebels were so far off that you could not distinguish a man from a mule with the naked eye, they would burst the shells over their works every time and scattering the deadly fragments right among

---

[15] Samuel D. Buck, "The Battle of Fisher's Hill," *Confederate Veteran* (November 1894): 338.

[16] For additional discussion of this phase of the fighting at Fisher's Hill see Noyalas, *The Battle of Fisher's Hill*, 64.

[17] Scott C. Patchan, "Fisher's Hill," *Blue & Gray Magazine* (Winter 2008): 22-26, 43-45; Barber Diary, September 22, 1864, JHL.

them. Scarcely a shot was thrown away, and yet it took them less time to sight their pieces than an ordinary hunter would take in aiming his rifle at a woodchuck."[18] In the battle's aftermath, Corporal Barber proudly wrote that Battery G "silenced their [the Confederates'] thunder."[19]

As the pressure from the infantry assault and artillery forced Early's army to retreat, Battery G kept up a "hot fire" with case shot until the Confederates were out of range. By battle's end Battery G fired 218 rounds of ammunition. While the battery reported no loss of human life, two of the battery's horses were killed.

Following the Battle of Fisher's Hill, the Army of the Shenandoah continued up the Valley to Harrisonburg. At various points during the march southward Battery G and the First New York Battery engaged elements of Early's command. Each time an enemy force was located, the guns were unlimbered and a few rounds thrown toward their position. Corporal Barber was there as he constantly sighted his number three gun. "Our Battery galloped on after them untill [*sic*] we come up with them and then open fire until they was out of range and then chase them again which was fun for us and death for them." Occasionally the Confederates would counter and attempt to stop the Rhode Islanders. The results were the same every time. "Our Battery fired a few rounds of case shot in among the brave rebel artillerymen and they got out of the way."[20]

Because the cannoneers did not always receive their full complement of supplies, they took ample opportunity to forage through the countryside. Private Horace Tanner of Hopkinton recorded, "I have helped myself to anything I have found in the enemies country without liberty or license and all the rest of the boys have done the same. We have consumed or destroyed everything we have come in contact with in the line of subsistence for man or beast." On one occasion, the men took 118 sheep. The actions of Sheridan's command in seizing livestock and foodstuffs,

---

[18] Wilbur Fisk, *Hard Marching Every Day: The Civil War Letters of Private Wilbur Fisk, 1861-1865* (Lawrence: University Press of Kansas, 1992), 257-260.

[19] Hartwell, et. al., *To My Beloved Wife*, 287-290; Barber Diary, September 22, 1864, JHL.

[20] Barber Diary, September 23-27, 1864, JHL; Bartlett, *Memoirs of Rhode Island*, 380-381.

the destruction of the Burning in late September and early October, and the victories at Winchester and Fisher's Hill demoralized the Valley's Confederate civilian population.[21] By October 10 the Army of the Shenandoah established camps along the banks of Cedar Creek, south of Middletown. Confidence soared among Sheridan's veterans, despite a fight near Hupp's Hill on October 13, that Early no longer proved a threat in the Shenandoah Valley. Two days later Sheridan departed the Valley for a conference with war planners in Washington, D.C. Although Sheridan believed Early proved no significant threat to his command, he maintained communication with General Wright, placed in temporary command during Sheridan's absence, to make certain that the army that had achieved so much over the past month was not placed in a vulnerable position.[22]

At the time Sheridan departed for Washington, the Army of the Shenandoah appeared to be in a strong position. The Eighth Corps guarded the army's left flank, the Nineteenth Corps held the center, and the Sixth Corps stood on the army's right flank. Sheridan also posted cavalry on both flanks. In order to protect the Sixth Corps' camp, Colonel Tompkins placed three of his rifled batteries on the east side of the line directly to the right of Belle Grove. Battery C, First Rhode Island held the right of the line, Adams' Battery G protected the center, and the Fifth Maine Battery guarded the left. The 121st New York, which supported the Rhode Islanders at Mine Run and Cool Spring, was detached from the first division assigned to support the artillery.[23]

Although confident Early would not strike, his army maneuvered throughout the night of October 18, and in the early hours of October 19 Early's Army of the Valley, shrouded in an early morning fog, slammed into the Army of the Shenandoah's right

---

[21] For further discussion of the impact of this see Jonathan A. Noyalas, *The Battle of Cedar Creek: Victory from the Jaws of Defeat* (Charleston, SC: History Press, 2009), 18. For the most detailed examination of the Burning see John L. Heatwole, *The Burning: Sheridan in the Shenandoah Valley* (Charlottesville, VA: Rockbridge Publishing, 1998).

[22] For additional discussion see Noyalas, *The Battle of Cedar Creek*, 24-25.

[23] Merritt, "Sheridan in the Shenandoah," 513-517; Barber Diary, October 15-18, 1864, JHL; Augustus C. Buell, *The Cannoneer* (Washington, DC: National Tribune, 1890), 283.

flank.[24] As troops from Confederate general Joseph Kershaw's division attacked Union colonel Joseph Thoburn's division, Corporal James Barber of Battery G was asleep in a shelter tent. Initially, Barber believed the sound of gunfire was nothing more than some inexperienced recruits firing at a noise they heard in the woods. All of a sudden, a heavy crash of musketry echoed through the still morning air that let the experienced combat veteran know that it was something more. Barber hastily packed up his equipment and ran to his gun. As the sound of battle intensified, awakening others, the Sixth Corps' battery commanders ordered all of their wagons, forges, and other non-combat vehicles to the rear. Throughout the encampment, the buglers sounded "Boots and Saddles." After roll call the men quickly packed up their belongings and threw them onto the caissons. While all of this happened the Eighth Corps gave way and eventually, despite resisting the Confederate onslaught for more than one hour, so too did General William Emory's Nineteenth Corps. With two of the army's infantry corps fleeing north, only the Sixth Corps remained to slow Early's assault.[25]

Corporal James Barber fought bravely at Cedar Creek.
He earned the Medal of Honor for his conduct at Petersburg on April 2, 1865
(*Courtesy Robert Grandchamp private collection*)

[24] For a more detailed examination of the opening Confederate attack at Cedar Creek see Noyalas, *The Battle of Cedar Creek*, 32-39.
[25] Scott C. Patchan, "Cedar Creek," *Blue and Gray Magazine* (Summer 2007): 40-41; Noyalas, *The Battle of Cedar Creek*, 48.

As the Confederates from Pegram's and Ramseur's divisions crossed Meadow Brook, the Sixth Corps' cannon stood directly in their path. Colonel Tompkins galloped through the camp trying to get his men to their posts, all the while seeing what was coming toward him. He ordered Captain Adams and Lieutenant Jacob Lamb, commanding Batteries G and C of Rhode Island respectively, to hold their position at all costs as the rest of the Sixth Corps was organized. The Rhode Islanders were to sacrifice themselves to the enemy to buy the precious time needed to prevent a total rout of the Army of the Shenandoah. Before doing so, they had to move the guns out of the depression in which they were camped and moved to a piece of higher ground to the rear. General Ramseur saw the artillery to his front and directed General Cullen Battle's brigade to attack. Lieutenant Colonel Edwin Hobson of the Fifth Alabama wrote of this moment: "I soon got permission to attack the battery that was playing upon us. Upon giving the order to the brigade to storm and take the battery the men bounded forward with a yell and in a few moments they were in the midst of the artillery calling upon the Yankees to surrender and when failing to do so cutting them down with their swords or shooting them down. We then captured six pieces of arty. The enemy defended manfully this battery & yielded possession of it to us only after the 5th Ala & portion of the 6th Ala Rgt were answering the guns." As Battle's Alabamians stormed in among the guns and caissons, the artillerists scrambled to their positions.[26]

Musician William H. Lewis was among the members of Battery G already at his post, galloping on his horse and blowing bugle calls for the drivers to mount and begin moving. As the enemy approached the battery, Lewis leaped from his own mount onto the lead team of one of the pairs of horses that was already harnessed and began to get the gun moving. Only a moment later, an Alabamian leveled his musket and pulled the trigger. Lewis fell off the horse to the ground, shot through the chest as two comrades grabbed him and raced for the rear; he died two days later. Although mortally wounded, Lewis "saved the gun from being

---

[26] Patchan, "Cedar Creek," 40-41; *O.R.* ser. I, vol. 43, 276-278; Edwin Hobson, Report of Cedar Creek, Cedar Creek Battlefield Foundation Collection, Middletown, VA (items from this collection hereafter cited as CCBF).

captured." One piece was moving to the right and safety, three more needed to follow.[27]

The scene in the artillery park was unbelievable; horses and artillerists were being shot down at an immense rate as they tried to move the guns. The fog, with the sound of battle, created a terrifying, ethereal atmosphere. Surgeon George T. Stevens of the 77th New York recorded: "They rushed our lines with those wild, exultant yells, the terror of which can never be conceived by those who have not heard them on the field." Private Charles G. Gardner of Battery G was on detached duty at the Sixth Corps Artillery Brigade headquarters. Gardner tried desperately to evacuate the brigade's medical wagons, but was killed in the process. Lieutenant John Knight Bucklyn of Colonel Tompkins' staff galloped through the camps transferring orders to get the batteries moving. The lieutenant rode through a hurricane of lead as the Alabamians fired into the camp. In the middle of their field of fire was Battery G. Corporal Barber who was among the first to join in the fight. As he looked into the fog, he saw, "advancing Rebels who came rushing onto our Battery yelling like the devil and firing as they come."[28]

Private James McDonald of Providence was mortally wounded by a shot through the lung. Another man with the same name, but from Richmond, Rhode Island, was wounded in the leg. James Matteson received a disfiguring wound to the face. Minié balls splintered the gun carriages and some made the distinct and frightening sound of hitting bone. To Corporal Barber, the projectiles sounded like hailstones "and the air seemed to be full of them." Finally, Lieutenant Bucklyn's horse was shot down as he carried on the mission on foot to get the guns moving. Private Thomas Harper, a Canadian immigrant from Providence was hit, but still ran for his life. The Confederates now took possession of the entire encampment, getting between the guns and shelter tents still standing; they fired at anything that moved. Panicked men continued to stream past Battery G as the drivers and cannoneers

---

[27] Henry Seamans to Mrs. Lewis, October 21 and November 30, 1864, Connecticut State Library, Hartford, CT.

[28] John K. Bucklyn, *Battle of Cedar Creek* (Providence, RI: Sydney S. Rider, 1883), 11-13. George T. Stevens, *Three Years in the Sixth Corps.* (New York: D. Van Nostrand, 1870), 419-420; Thomas W. Bicknell, *A History of Barrington, Rhode Island* (Providence, RI: Snow and Farnum, 1898), 507. Barber Diary, October 19, 1864, JHL.

remained by their places. Adams had trained his men well, they did not run, but tried in every way to save their guns from the enemy. Battle's Alabamians and another brigade of Georgians were soon almost on top of the battery. Corporal Henry E. Chace of Westerly, the brother of First Sergeant Nathaniel Chace, was killed at his post.[29]

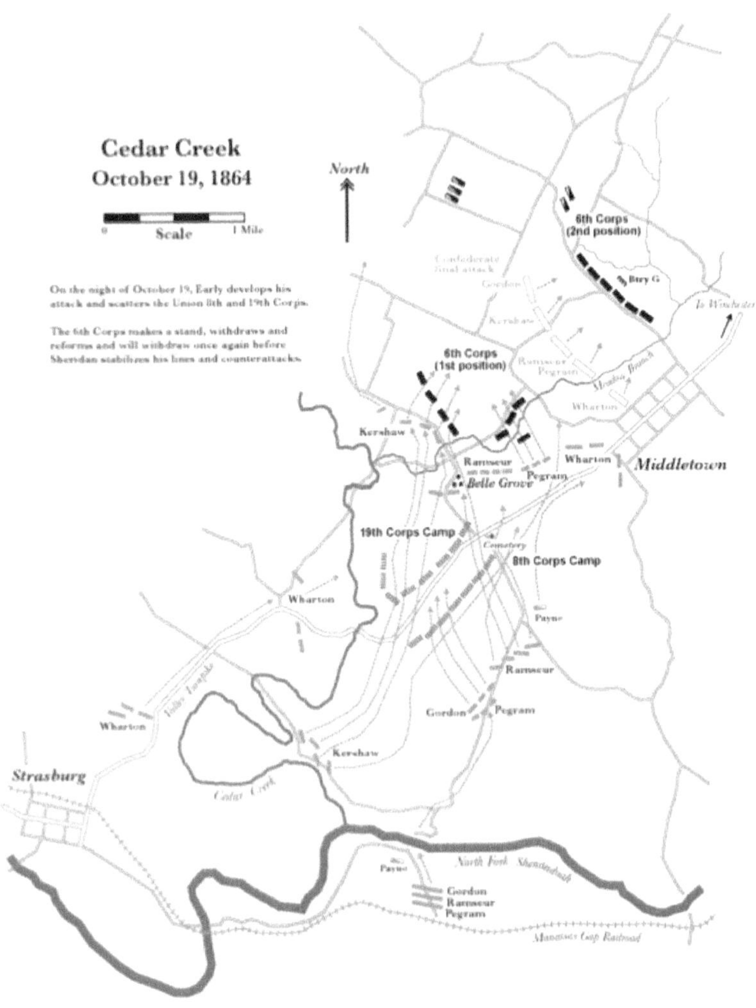

Map of the Battle of Cedar Creek
(*Courtesy Robert Grandchamp*)

---

[29] *Narragansett Weekly,* November 10, 1864; Abijah P. Marvin, *History of Winchendon* (Winchendon, MA: N.P., 1868), 506.

In the tight, compact area of the artillery brigade's encampment the soldiers in Battery G received a tremendous fire. A few of the artillerists tried to form a skirmish line and return fire with their revolvers, but it accomplished nothing as the Alabamians continued to fire at the Rhode Islanders. Most soon abandoned this plan and ran back to their guns, trying in vain to get them moving. Sergeant Alexander Sisson and his twin brother, Charles, were both hit, while John S. Babcock was severely wounded in the legs as he helped to evacuate their gun. Private Edward Forrest lost his nerve and skedaddled to the rear; he would rejoin the command the following day. While the enlisted men were trying to perform their duty, the officers did all humanly possible to stem the Confederate onslaught. As Lieutenant Charles V. Scott, only recently returned to the unit after suffering a severe wound at Cold Harbor, ran to his section the young officer was shot in the left knee and right thigh. Scott's men carried him to a wagon for treatment before returning to the guns. Scott died one month later.[30]

Lt. Charles V. Scott
(*Courtesy Robert Grandchamp private collection*)

---

[30] Buell, *The Cannoneer,* 300-301. *Narragansett Weekly,* November 10, 1864. Charles V. Scott, Compiled Service Record, National Archives and Records Administration, Washington, D.C.

As the horses were being shot down all around him, Captain Adams and two other men, Corporal Daniel Hoxsie and an unidentified private, were trying to get one of the guns moving: three Rhode Islanders trying to push a ton of iron and wood. The *Providence Journal* called the act one of "unsurpassed bravery." The Confederates had already killed all the gun's horses. Now Corporal Hoxsie, recently recovered from a wound he received at Cold Harbor, was shot in the leg; this was the third wound he had received up to this point in the conflict. Also wounded was the unidentified private. Other Rhode Islanders were quickly on the scene and rescued their two comrades, while leaving the gun to the enemy. Hoxsie languished in a hospital in Washington and would not be discharged until the following August. Finally, Colonel Tompkins dismounted and, with one of his captains, tried to push the gun out of harm's way. The colonel received a wound to the arm that took him out of active field service for the rest of the war. Tompkins received a promotion to brevet of brigadier general for his services in the 1864 Shenandoah Campaign. Privates Nathan and Samuel Chaplin, brothers from Westerly, also tried to save the battery, but were shot in the process.[31]

With no other support, Captain Adams was forced to abandon two guns and two caissons as he ran to join the remaining one piece already moving on, the only one to have its horses left, which had been saved by William Lewis. The captain left just in time as the Confederates were "up nearly to the muzzles of our guns." The worst fear of a cannoneer had been realized. Battery G lost two of its guns. While Adams had been grasping to save one gun, gunners were in the process of preparing to drag another off the field. The men were fortunate to save two of their pieces. Captain Hazard Stevens, a transplanted Rhode Islander on General Wright's staff wrote, "Only by great bravery and steadiness was any of the artillery saved. Every man seemed to be doing his best, and more acts of courage and desperation have seldom been scene [*sic*]." As the Rhode Islanders left, three of their comrades remained behind severely wounded; they were promptly taken prisoner by the Confederates.[32]

---

[31] *Providence Journal,* October 24, 1864; Bartlett, *Memoirs of Rhode Island,* 381-382.
[32] *Narragansett Weekly,* November 10, 1864; Hazard Stevens, "The Battle of Cedar Creek: October 19, 1864," *Civil War Papers Read before the Commandery*

The full force of two Confederate divisions was directed against the Sixth Corps' encampments. "The firing became very hot," recorded Corporal Barber who continued to fight on with his detachment. The 121st New York had been on the firing line, trying in vain to hold back the Confederate assault. Now the New Yorkers obliqued to the left and charged towards the artillery to lend support. Forming a line near the two Rhode Island batteries, they managed to hold the Confederates at bay long enough, while the artillerists finally managed to get the other gun moving. The Confederates tried to make one last effort to take the guns, but the New Yorkers fired a murderous volley as the second cannon was pulled out by hand. Private John D. Ingraham recalled, "We poured it into them wicked, which checked them for a while." Some of the infantry threw down their muskets and helped the Rhode Islanders pull their gun out of the cauldron. So many horses were dead that this was the only way to withdraw. The 121st New York suffered heavy losses but managed to hold out long enough to cover the withdrawal. As the guns were withdrawn, clumps of dead and wounded New Yorkers, Alabamians, and Rhode Islanders were left among the wreckage of the camp. Colonel Tompkins recalled, "The guns were not deserted by their gunners, but were heroically worked and defended until nearly every man fell at his post."[33]

Once Captain Adams was positive that there was no Union infantry to the front of his guns, he gave the order for canister as Battery G began to fight back against the onslaught. The section wheeled to the right and helped to stem the flow of the Sixth Corps to the rear. The Alabamians came under a destructive fire but continued to advance. The remnants of Lamb's Battery joined in the fight to Battery G's left, as the Vermont Brigade launched a desperate charge to their right to save Captain James McKnight's Battery M, 5th United States Artillery. What was left of Colonel William Penrose's New Jersey Brigade supported the efforts to cover Battery G's withdrawal, all the while pulling back under a

----

of the State of Massachusetts, Military Order of the Loyal Legion of the United States, Volume I (Boston: E.H. Gilson, 1900), 206-207.

[33] Isaac O. Best, *History of the 121st New York State Infantry* (Chicago: James H. Smith, 1921), 193-198; Bartlett, *Memoirs of Rhode Island,* 381-382; John D. Ingraham to Parents, October 23, 1864, CCBF; Hartwell, et. al., *To My Beloved Wife,* 298-300; Barber Diary, October 19, 1864, JHL. According to Ingraham, the 121st New York lost fifty men in its stand.

destructive fire. The results of the canister fire were seen immediately. "Our guns belched forth their thunder, firing heavy charges of canister in the midst of the advancing Rebels," recorded Corporal Barber. To their front the men watched on as their fire tore huge gaps into the advancing lines, knocking down a Confederate color bearer; still Early's army kept on advancing.[34]

Even the Confederates who were trying to capture Battery G could not believe the bravery displayed by the Rhode Islanders. Although the cannoneers and drivers continued to be shot down, they refused to yield their ordnance rifles, which had served them on every battlefield since the Peninsula Campaign. Benjamin F. Cobb, 10th Georgia Infantry, a regiment which along with the 5th and 6th Alabama Infantry, rushed to capture the Sixth Corps artillery, remembered: "The order was furnished and we marched up a hill about one hundred yards with a battery shelling us from the time we struck their picket line at the creek. But they did us very little damage until we got to the top of the hill. I remarked to Lt. [J.C.] Hendron, who was marching by my side, saying look out we are going to catch it and just at that time the whole line opened fire on us. That really done us more damage than all the balance of the days fighting. Killed and wounded scores of our boys. But that was all the licks they got at us, there we gave a Rebel yell and ran right in on them and scattered them like chaff before the wind." The Rhode Islanders continued to fight and the next blast of canister severely wounded Cobb and Hendron as they made one last attempt to get to the two guns.[35]

Although the battery had suffered heavily, it was making its presence known to the Confederates who had attacked it. Colonel Edwin Lafayette Hobson of Alabama wrote, "The brigade was exposed to withering and accurate shelling from a battery of the enemy distant about three hundred yards and obliquely to the left. The men behaved with unequalled calmness while those shells were rapidly thinning their ranks." To their front, the artillerists could see the other two guns that were abandoned, but many in the

---

[34] Barber Diary, October 19, 1864, JHL; Bucklyn, *Battle of Cedar Creek,* 13-15; Stevens, *Three Years in the Sixth Corps,* 419; Alanson Haines, *History of the Fifteenth Regiment New Jersey Volunteers* (New York: Jenkins & Thomas, Printers, 1883), 276-278.
[35] Benjamin F. Cobb, "My Last Battle," CCBF.

ranks yelled out, "We will retake those guns before night." Much to the horror of the soldiers in the Sixth Corps, not only had the Confederates captured the guns, but they were swarming over them, readying the pieces to fire on Union troops. The two ordnance rifles of Battery G were turned on the battery by the enemy. Private William H. Burton had already been wounded at Marye's Heights; now he was hit again.[36]

Battery G was not the only Sixth Corps battery to suffer terribly; most had lost many of their horses and could pull only two guns out, while leaving many men behind to the enemy. As Battery M, 5th United States Artillery was drawn back by hand, Corporal Augustus Buell looked in the distance and saw the overwhelming fight against the Rhode Islanders. He wrote that Battery G, "Got into a hot place and was made the subject of a regular rough-and-tumble between Upton's Brigade and a strong force of the enemy. The Rebels got into the battery once, but were driven out of it. Then their second line took it again. They got away, but nearly all their men and horses were killed or disabled."[37]

Under the tremendous fire power being thrown against the Sixth Corps, few of the infantrymen who had been fighting alongside Battery G remained on the field; they had either been killed or fled north. Meanwhile, the Rhode Islanders continued their mission to save their two remaining ordnance rifles. The situation was now more than desperate for Captain Adams as a third of his men were lost and only a few rounds remained in the limber chests. All of a sudden through the white sulfuric smoke of battle, the Rhode Islanders saw a most welcome sight. It was a brigade of men with white Greek crosses and sprigs of evergreen in their hats—the Vermont Brigade, which Battery G had supported on several occasions. The Green Mountain Boys held firm, ready to repay the services rendered by the artillerymen. Now they stood on a hill with leveled Enfield muskets ready to fire at the advancing foe as soon as Battery G was clear from their field of fire. The Rhode Islanders had done their duty; they had stymied the flow of retreat, but at a huge price. General Frank Wheaton witnessed Battery G's

---

[36] Hobson, Report of Cedar Creek, CCBF; Frederick D. Bidwell, *History of the Forty-Ninth New York Volunteers* (Albany: J.B. Lyon, 1916), 74-76; *Narragansett Weekly*, November 10, 1864.
[37] Buell, *The Cannoneer,* 306.

stand and wrote, "I never saw a battery more ably and desperately fought."[38]

For two hours, the Sixth Corps put up a heroic fight, grudgingly trading ground as they delayed the Confederates. Battery G withdrew a mile and a half under fire. Finally, satisfied he had driven the enemy from the field, General Early halted the attack. His subordinates pleaded with him to renew the initiative, but Early refused. Now the Army of the Shenandoah had an opportunity to regroup. Colonel Tompkins returned to the field and ordered the batteries to change ammunition chests for the struggle which he believed would be renewed.

Around 10:00 a.m. General Sheridan arrived from Winchester and assured his command that they would regain all that had been lost during the morning's fight.[39] Approximately six hours later the Army of the Shenandoah launched its counterattack. The artillery acted much as it did at Fisher's Hill, working with the infantry to drive back the enemy on the front line. Although they had been decimated in the early morning fight, Battery G again went into combat for twenty minutes with its two guns, using the case shot that remained in the limber chests, shelling the fleeing Confederates and their wagon train that had become bogged down on the Valley Pike. Captain Stevens wrote, "Adams' G Battery maintained a rapid and effective fire until the

---

[38] Joseph G. Bilby, *Three Rousing Cheers: A History of the Fifteenth New Jersey from Flemington to Appomattox* (Hightstown, NJ: Longstreet House, 2001), 206-207; Bartlett, *Memoirs of Rhode Island*, 381-382, 416.

[39] Noyalas, *The Battle of Cedar Creek*, 60. It is not the purpose of this essay to rehash all aspects of the Battle of Cedar Creek, however, Sheridan's arrival on the field around 10 a.m.—the culmination of his ride from Winchester— proved a critical moment in the battle, in the shaping of Sheridan's legacy, and in the postwar fighting among Union veterans about what they believed turned the tide at Cedar Creek. For discussion of the ride and the postwar bickering that ensued see Jonathan A. Noyalas, "'Its Thrill Will Never Die': Sheridan's Ride in War and Memory" in *"We Learned that We are Indivisible": Sesquicentennial Reflections on the Civil War Era in the Shenandoah Valley*, eds. Jonathan A. Noyalas and Nancy T. Sorrells (Newcastle upon Tyne, UK: Cambridge Scholars, 2015), 143-167; Jonathan A. Noyalas, " 'It is Natural That Each Comrade Should Think His Corps the Best': Sheridan's Veterans Refight the 1864 Shenandoah Campaign" in *The War Went On: Reconsidering the Lives of Civil War Veterans*, eds. Brian Matthew Jordan and Evan C. Rothera (Baton Rouge: Louisiana State University Press, 2020), 167-169.

enemy gave way." By dusk it was the Confederates who were running. The fierce counterattack won the day and an unbelievable victory for the Union cause.[40]

With the battle over, the exhausted survivors of the Sixth Corps Artillery Brigade simply wanted to eat a meal and go to sleep, but sounds of bugle calls filled the air summoning them to their posts. Sheridan's cavalry captured forty-eight artillery pieces from the Confederates; Sheridan wanted them removed from the field immediately. In Battery G, the men were anxious to perform the duty as they finally retook the two guns lost earlier in the day. The cannoneers worked all night to drag in the pieces and recover wounded comrades. As they cleared the field, the artillerists were sickened. Even though the Confederates retreated, they had stripped the dead of their clothing and equipment, leaving behind a ghastly scene. The fallen of Battery G were spared such a fate. That night the men in Battery G lay down to sleep in their old camp; some things would never be the same. Many comrades who had served for nearly three years never returned to duty or found a soldier's grave. Corporal James Barber wrote, "This has been a day which shall live in history and one long to be remembered by those who took part in this engagement."[41]

The Sixth Corps Artillery Brigade suffered heavily. In total 130 artillerists were hit, a third of the brigade. Two thirds of the horses were also dead. The scene was sobering to even the most battle-hardened veteran. After surviving the carnage of Antietam, Gettysburg, and the Overland Campaign, one veteran confessed: "All the batteries of the Sixth Corps suffered heavily." Of the losses, nearly half were Rhode Islanders; Battery G had the highest number of casualties in the brigade. To hurt the pride of the cannoneers, there were twenty-four pieces in camp, of which seven were captured and later retaken. That night General Wright rode up to the shattered command and personally thanked Captain Adams and his battery for their performance in the battle, claiming they had saved many lives by their fighting retreat. Another officer summed up Battery G's performance by stating they had "rendered

---

[40] Bartlett, *Memoirs of Rhode Island,* 381-382; Stevens, "Cedar Creek," 230-231; Buell, *The Cannoneer,* 301-302.
[41] Bucklyn, *Cedar Creek,* 20-23; Barber Diary, October 19, 1864, JHL.

effective service."[42]

The officers and men of Adams' Battery obeyed Colonel Tompkins' orders to stay and fight; the cost however was more than could be burdened by one small command from the nation's smallest state. Battery G had suffered the second highest loss for a Rhode Island battery in the war; only ninety officers and men had been engaged in the battle. Of these, nine soldiers were killed or mortally wounded, while twenty-three were wounded. Of the wounded, three men were captured and sent to Richmond as prisoners-of-war. Among the dying was Private Simeon Starboard, a substitute, who unlike many other substitutes remained in the service. Starboard had only recently returned from being sick in Washington, where he still owed the sutlers $16. The men in Westerly's First Detachment again lost the most; two were killed and seven were wounded. One of the injured from the town was Private Samuel W. Place, who had been hit in the lower right leg. The surgeons had no choice but to amputate and try to save his life before gangrene set in. The operation was successful and Place survived.[43]

Four of the wounded in the battery had been hit at both Marye's Heights and now at Cedar Creek. As much a part of the battery as the cannoneers and drivers, another group of battery members suffered horrendous losses, the horses. Forty-five of the battery's horses died at Cedar Creek. Battery G lost one third of its strength at Cedar Creek: almost unheard of for an artillery battery. There was no rest for the artillerists the day after the battle. Following a brief meal, the battery went back to the battlefield and performed the solemn task of burying the four men who were killed

---

[42] Bartlett, *Memoirs of Rhode Island*, 381-382, 416; *Providence Journal*, October 14, 1883; Buell, *The Cannoneer*, 306; *The Union Army: A History of Military Affairs in the Loyal States 1861-65-Records of the Regiments in the Union Army-Cyclopedia of Battles-Memoirs of Commanders and Soldiers: Volume I, Maine, New Hampshire, Vermont, Massachusetts, Rhode Island, Connecticut, Pennsylvania, and Delaware* (Wilmington, NC: Broadfoot Publishing, 1997), 254.

[43] Battery G, Morning Report, October 20, 1864, National Archives and Records Administration, Washington, D.C.; Simeon Starboard, Compiled Service Record, National Archives and Records Administration, Washington, D.C.; Charles Tompkins to Edward C. Mauran, November 14, 1864, Rhode Island State Archives, Providence, RI. *The Medical and Surgical History of the War of the Rebellion* (Washington: Government Printing Office, 1883) I: 295.

in action. With this completed the battery received additional ammunition to replace what was expended in the battle.[44]

As usual, the people of Rhode Island had only a fleeting glance of what happened to Battery G at Cedar Creek. The *Providence Journal*, on October 24, presented a small paragraph about Captain Adams' attempt to evacuate the cannon. Three days later the paper printed the standard casualty list, forwarded by a member of the command. Private Thomas L. Stillman of Westerly wrote two letters to the local *Narragansett Weekly*. One headline was, "Rhode Island Battery G appears to have had warm work in the battle of Cedar Creek." The second was a listing of the many casualties the battery had suffered, with a special emphasis on the majority from south-western Rhode Island, where nearly a third of Battery G had been recruited. The general lack of coverage of the battle was not only of concern to the Rhode Islanders, but to all of the soldiers who fought through it. A Massachusetts soldier in the Sixth Corps wrote, "We have no Newspapers to blow for this corps."[45]

In Westerly, the way of life had continued much the same throughout the war, except too many of the young men in the town were gone. The Civil War brought great economic benefits to Westerly. The town became a commercial and transportation hub as the many mills produced the rough kersey cloth for soldiers' trousers and blankets. The many local farms had continued to produce food for the Union war effort. Now, after yet another harvest, the third since Battery G left, two of Westerly's sons were never coming home. Corporal Henry Chace and Private William C. Douglass had been killed at Cedar Creek. Unlike most Westerly soldiers who died in the conflict, their bodies were left in the South and not returned to River Bend or to a cemetery on their own property. The only solace that Archibald Chace could take was a letter from Captain Adams relating that his son Henry "performed

---

[44] Battery G, Morning Report, October 20, 1864, National Archives and Records Administration, Washington, D.C.; Tompkins to Mauran, November 14, 1864, Rhode Island State Archives, Providence, RI.

[45] *Providence Journal*, October 24, 1864, October 27, 1864; *Narragansett Weekly*, October 27, 1864, November 10, 1864; John S. Collier and Bonnie B. Collier, eds., *Yours for the Union: The Civil War Letters of John W. Chase, First Massachusetts Light Artillery* (New York: Fordham University Press, 2004), 369-372.

his duty faithfully, and was loved by everyone." Archibald Chace could take pride in the fact that his surviving son, Nathaniel Ray, had not only survived the engagement but had earned a rare battlefield promotion and was on his way to join Battery B.[46]

Corporal Henry E. Chace's tombstone in the Winchester National Cemetery.
(*Photo by Robert Grandchamp*)

Unlike other fields of battle where Rhode Island artillerymen fought and died, there was never a memorial erected at Cedar Creek. Rather the forgotten words of Colonel Charles Tompkins in a letter to Governor James Y. Smith is the enduring legacy of Battery G's stand at Cedar Creek: "The conduct of officers and men was gallant in the extreme and it merits the hearty commendation of all who witnessed it. Rhode Island has just cause to be proud of such soldiers."[47]

Among the many promotions that were given out to Battery G for their stand at Cedar Creek was one to Captain George Adams. General Wheaton was amazed at Adams' handling of his battery at Cedar Creek and wrote several letters calling for his promotion. "In

---

[46] *Narragansett Weekly,* November 10, 1864; Marvin, *History of Winchendon,* 506.
[47] Tompkins to Mauran, November 14, 1864, Rhode Island State Archives, Providence, RI.

my opinion he has few superiors in the service, and his admirable battery has been so skillfully and gallantly handled in battle." General Wright added, "Captain Adams is not only thoroughly competent to discharge the duties of an advanced grade, but had claims for promotion earned on many a hard-fought field, and I am only discharging my duty in commending him." The two letters were forwarded to Sheridan's headquarters; the commanding general apparently had heard of Adams' actions as he affixed his own endorsement before sending the letters to Secretary of War Edward Stanton. Stanton acted upon the recommendations and Adams received a brevet to major in November.[48]

After remaining in the Shenandoah Valley for five months, Grant ordered the Sixth Corps back to Petersburg in late November. Battery G was not going with their parent organization; however, they were sent to Washington to refit and to consolidate with Battery C, First Rhode Island Light Artillery, which had also lost heavily at Cedar Creek. Captain Adams and his men returned to Petersburg in February 1865. On April 2, 1865, during the Sixth Corps' assault on the Confederate lines, Captain Adams and a party of his men volunteered to accompany the assaulting infantry column. Rushing the enemy line, they captured two enemy howitzers which were then turned around and used on the fleeing Confederates in what was called "One of the most perilous exploits of the Rebellion." For their actions that day, seven men from Battery G, including Corporal James Barber, were awarded the Medal of Honor. Adams received two brevets for his heroism. Mustered out in June 1865, Battery G returned to Rhode Island. As his last official act as commander of Battery G, Captain and Brevet Colonel George W. Adams turned the tattered, battle worn guidon into the custody of the State of Rhode Island for safe keeping for posterity. Proudly inscribed on the banner were the honors: Opequon, Fisher's Hill, and Cedar Creek.[49]

---

[48] Bartlett, *Memoirs of Rhode Island*, 416-417.
[49] For the most comprehensive history of Battery G, refer to Robert Grandchamp, *The Boys of Adams' Battery G: The Civil War through the Eyes of a Union Light Artillery Unit* (Jefferson, NC: McFarland, 2009).

"A Division Whose Record Tells of Nothing but Success"

General William Woods Averell & His Cavalry Division at the Third Battle of Winchester

Scott C. Patchan

Brigadier General William Woods Averell and his division went into the Third Battle of Winchester as a question mark among the mounted arm of Major General Phillip H. Sheridan's Army of the Shenandoah. After being deposed from the Army of the Potomac on the heels of a poor showing during the Chancellorsville Campaign, the New York born Averell had performed well since joining the Department of West Virginia. He especially excelled as an independent commander at Droop Mountain in November 1863; Rutherford's Farm on July 20, 1864; and at Moorefield, West Virginia, on August 7, 1864. Yet during the same period he exhibited difficulties in successfully coordinating his command as part of a larger force. Averell, it seems, chaffed under close direction and supervision. Major General David Hunter lamented the trust he had placed in Averell during the Lynchburg Campaign, and Major General George Crook agreed with Hunter's assessment. Averell further annoyed Crook with a subpar performance at the Second Battle of Kernstown on July 24, which Crook unfairly used to scapegoat Averell for the Union defeat at that battle. In his largely self-serving memoirs, Crook went so far as to perpetuate rumors of Averell being intoxicated on that occasion.[1]

Crook's negative impressions of Averell took on greater meaning when Sheridan received command of the U. S. Army of

---

[1] Martin Schmidt, ed., *General George Crook: His Autobiography* (Norman, OK: University of Oklahoma Press, 1960), 123.

the Shenandoah. Crook, an old friend of Sheridan, quickly became one of the new army commander's closest confidantes. Crook almost certainly did not express favorable opinions of Averell. Sheridan chose to retain Averell, but the New Yorker quickly became his own enemy. Averell moved slowly in returning his division from his successful battle at Moorefield. On August 9, Averell then at New Creek, West Virginia, received orders from Sheridan to concentrate his division and "join me by the shortest and most practicable route." It took Averell five days to reach Martinsburg and shortly after arriving he learned that Major General Alfred Torbert, previously a division commander in the Army of the Potomac's Cavalry Corps under Sheridan, had been appointed commander of all cavalry in the Shenandoah Valley on August 9. Averell held senior rank over Torbert and complained about this slight. Averell later complained, "Major General Sheridan illegally assumed the prerogative of the President of the United States and ordered me to report to a junior officer on the 23d of August without any just cause." What Averell did not understand was that General Ulysses S. Grant had advised Sheridan on August 7, "Do not hesitate to give commands to officers in whom you repose confidence, without regard to claims of others on account of rank. If you deem Torbert the best man to command the cavalry, place him in command and give Averell some other command or relieve him." Sheridan kept Averell as a division commander for the interim but one of Averell's brigade commanders, Colonel William H. Powell, recalled his commander's reaction to the situation: "At the selection of General Torbert as commander of the cavalry corps, Averell expressed great disappointment and chagrin, which developed in his disregard of orders that induced his removal from command" on September 23, 1864.[2]

The situation remained tenuous between Averell, Sheridan and Torbert with Averell receiving a series of confusing orders from both men. Averell appropriately followed them only to be questioned by Sheridan as to why he made those movements. The

---

[2] U.S. War Department, comp., *War of the Rebellion: A Compilation of the Official Records of the Union and Confederate Armies* (Washington, D.C.: U.S. Government Printing Office, 1880-1901), ser. 1, vol. 43, 500-501, 719 (hereafter cited as *O.R.*).

situation had no impact on the military situation but clearly underscored the tension that was brewing within Sheridan's cavalry. On September 1, U. S. Grant focused on Averell's withdrawals and wrote to Sheridan, "The frequent reports of Averell's fall back without much fighting and being able to take his old position without opposition, presents a very bad appearance at this distance. You can judge better of his merits than I can, but it looks to me as if it was time to try some other officer in his place. If you think as I do in this matter, relieve him at once and name his successor."[3] Grant's assessment was based upon a single instance of Averell abandoning Martinsburg on September 1 and then quickly reoccupying it. Nevertheless, Sheridan stayed with Averell. Averell afterward upped his game in the lead up to the Third Battle of Winchester. He continually threatened the Confederates in the Winchester area through harassing advances that drove back the Southern cavalry and forced the Southerners to deploy infantry to repel Averell.

The plan of battle for Winchester called for Averell to advance south from Martinsburg and meet Torbert on the Valley Pike as circumstances dictated. Then, Torbert would lead two divisions toward Winchester. So far in the month of September, Averell had acted in a relatively independent manner on the army's northern flank at distance from Torbert. With the advent of a major battle, Sheridan expected Averell to work under the immediate direction of Torbert in conjunction with the division of Brigadier General Wesley Merritt. While Merritt broke camp at 2:00 a.m. like most units in the army, Averell did not depart until 5:00 a.m. and seemed to have moved slowly in joining the action on September 19, while the balance of Torbert's command was engaged before sunrise. Averell began the day with his two brigades split, Colonel James Schoonmaker's command was in Martinsburg and Colonel William Powell was at Leetown about seven miles southeast of that town as the crow flies. The two brigades united at Darkesville, a small hamlet on the Valley Pike, eight miles south of Martinsburg.

At Darkesville, Averell's advance guard encountered its first resistance at 8:30 a.m. in the form of Colonel George Smith's Virginia cavalry brigade. While Averell had 2,500 men and a six-gun

---

[3] *O.R.,* ser. I, vol. 43, pt. 2, 3-4.

battery under his command, Smith had only 600 poorly armed and mounted troopers. The Union troopers easily shoved them back three miles to Bunker Hill where Smith made a more determined stand. Averell hoped to get in close and smash Smith's command, but recent experience had taught the poorly armed Virginians to avoid close encounters with Averell's men. Instead, the Confederates broke and retreated quickly toward Winchester, leaving the road open to Averell. Although encountering only token opposition, Averell halted at Bunker Hill and reorganized his division before continuing the advance. It would be several hours before his troops were in action again while Torbert and Merritt were battling a Confederate infantry division at Brucetown, a few miles to the south. From Averell's perspective, he had not received instructions from Torbert, but could clearly hear the sounds of a battle. Uncertain of the developing circumstances in his front, Averell chose to take a cautious approach.

General William Averell
(*Courtesy Library of Congress*)

Averell neared the area of Stephenson's Depot in the early afternoon, a development that prompted Confederate General John C. Breckinridge to withdraw his division from its position at Brucetown where he had pinned down Torbert and Merritt. As Breckinridge withdrew, he deployed a covering force of infantry and artillery and successfully checked Averell's advance. Under a heavy artillery fire, Averell's cavalrymen withdrew about a half mile behind a sheltering rise of ground. Breckinridge used the opportunity to withdraw all of his infantry and most artillery from the Stephenson's Depot area. Torbert and Merritt belatedly realized that only Colonel Milton Ferguson's Virginia cavalry was in their front and promptly attacked and drove it back toward the depot area. This action was largely handled by two brigades of Merritt's division. One small Virginia regiment and a battery kept the cautious Averell at bay, while Smith joined Ferguson in the effort against Merritt. Eventually, Averell charged the rear of some of the Confederates opposing Merritt and assisted in routing them. Torbert then halted and regrouped his two divisions on Rutherford's Farm, with Averell deploying west of the Pike and Merritt upon the road and to its east. Two small Confederate brigades reinforced Smith and Ferguson and the whole readied to receive the charge. The 6,000 Union horsemen easily routed the Southerners, although some plucky Virginians made a counter charge that temporarily dented the Union line before being overrun by the blue mass.

Averell encountered less resistance but moved cautiously. He sent a staff officer to Sheridan with a message that Averell "had been chasing the rebels in from Martinsburg and Bunker Hill all day." Sheridan issued orders for Averell to charge immediately, but the staff officer did his chief no favors. Rather, in manner that typified Averell's occasional balkiness, the staffer replied that their horses had been out for days and nights and could not move "faster than a walk." Sheridan exploded, "Tell him to charge. Tell him I say to charge. We've got the rebels on the hip... Do it quick. I don't care a ---- for horse flesh today!" Unfortunately for Averell, the aide's representation of the division's situation gave Sheridan a false impression of what was actually occurring on the battlefield. There, Averell's division was attacking under the direction of Torbert.[4]

---

[4] Scott C. Patchan, *The Last Battle of Winchester* (Eldorado Hills, CA: Savas

On Averell's sector of the battlefield, some confusion erupted as a small Confederate brigade moving from the west at one point was behind Averell and cut off from their comrades in his front. Averell's command, however, allowed it to escape. One Georgia horse soldier thought it "mysterious" that Averell's men did not attack the small isolated force of Confederates. Instead, the Confederates detoured to the west and formed on the left of the Confederate line. When the attack occurred, Averell routed the Confederates in his front and sent them reeling toward Winchester in confusion. Many of the Confederates rallied upon some artillery and dismounted troopers who had taken position behind a stone wall beyond a small stream about a half mile closer to Winchester. The Confederates brought Averell's command to bay, but the New Yorker turned to his only reserves, the 1st New York Lincoln Cavalry and put them in on a dismounted charge against the exposed eastern flank of that rebel line. At the same time, Colonel James Schoonmaker, commanding a brigade of Ohioans and Pennsylvanians, ordered a charge on the right directly at the stone wall. With the New Yorkers hitting the flank, Schoonmaker's men overran the position, capturing eighty prisoners and one piece of artillery. Simultaneously, Colonel William Powell's three West Virginia regiments surged forward closer to the Pike and with Merritt pursued other retreating Confederate forces toward Winchester.[5]

At this point, Averell's division charged across the rugged ground along the eastern base of a height that contained Star Fort, which was unoccupied at the time. Powell focused his brigade toward the pike with Merritt while Schoonmaker pursued the broken Confederates toward the next height to the south, Fort Hill. Here several fortifications existed, including Milroy's Fort built by the Federals in 1863 and Fort Jackson constructed by the Confederates in 1861 to resist an attack from the north. Some of the Confederates attempted to rally in the latter fort on this height, but Schoonmaker charged boldly, driving them out in confusion. Some elements of his brigade charged entirely across the heights and went into Winchester's outskirts going as far as the town's spring

---

Beatie, 2013), 365.
[5] John W. Lee, "Memories of the Virginia Valley Campaign of 1864," *The Georgia Enterprise*, February 19, 1904.

before realizing that they had become isolated. Rear echelon Confederate troops quickly gathered and opened fire at the troopers who quickly dashed back to safety with their main body.

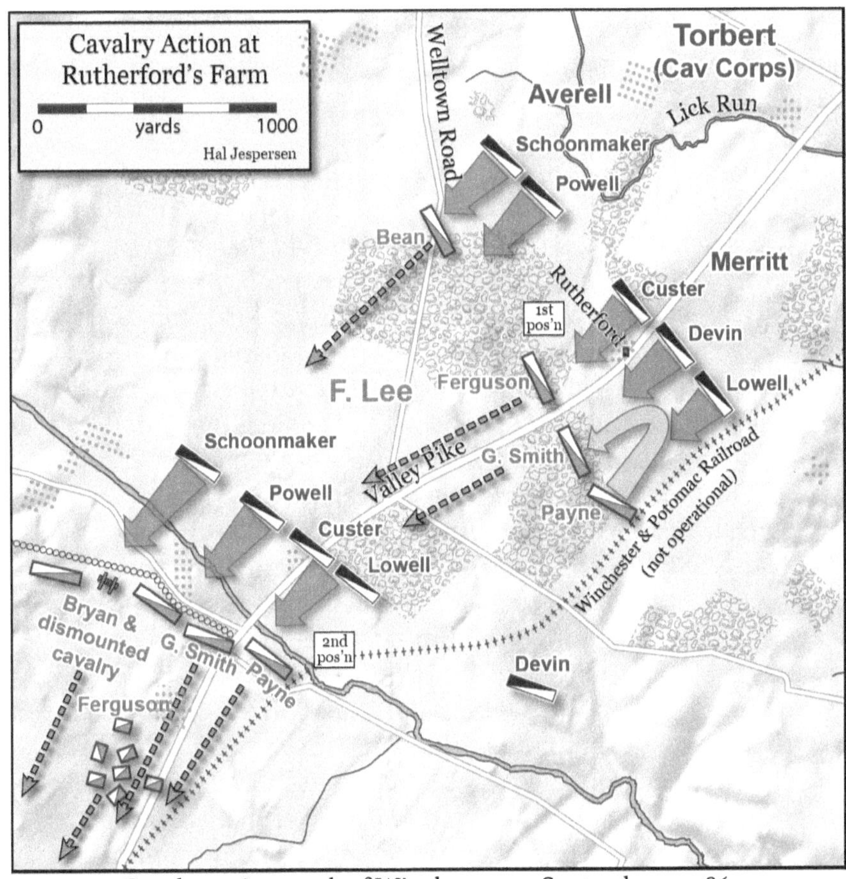

Cavalry action north of Winchester on September 19, 1864
(*Courtesy Scott C. Patchan*)

At this point, Torbert's cavalry had chased its Confederate counterparts over an extended distance and had lost its cohesiveness in its victorious jaunt. Confederate general Jubal Early had turned all of his artillery toward the Pike and directed General John C. Breckinridge to counterattack against Merritt with two infantry brigades. This sudden surge of firepower forced Merritt to fall back and regroup. Averell complained that his attack had "seized the heights west of town, and penetrated the town itself, when the giving away of Custer's brigade opened my left flank to the enemy's attack, an opportunity which he quickly embraced with artillery and infantry." Additionally, General Early had dispatched Colonel Thomas Munford with his Virginia brigade to secure Fort Hill. Munford arrived to find Schoonmaker's men scattered about the top of the heights and in possession of Fort Jackson. Munford recalled the scene:

> *Averill [sic] had sent a mounted regiment to take Fort Hill, to the north of Winchester, and a very commanding position to the west of the pike. General Early had no idea of allowing him to hold it, as that covered the pike below, and sent orders to me to take it and hold it. Up the hill we went and at them, followed by two guns of our horse artillery. We drove them from the hill, ran the two pieces in the fort, dismounted First, Second and Fourth Virginia cavalry, giving the Third Virginia the protection of the led horses, and we had just gotten well into the fort when Averill charged to recapture it; but we gave them a rough welcome, and sent them back faster than they came up.[6]*

Averell claimed that his division did not relinquish the ground he had gained, but he certainly was unable to retain control of Fort Hill. Contemporary Confederate sources, written and drawn, overwhelmingly reject the New Yorker's claim. Averell then claimed that only the attack by Crook's infantry carried the day and that some of his infantry came to Averell's assistance. In fact, Crook's infantry had been stalled after making significant progress, and it was the efforts of Merritt's regrouped division, aided by Powell's brigade of Averell's division, that smashed the Confederate left while the Sixth Army Corps joined the attack from the east, freeing Crook to resume his advance. Sheridan, however, heaped the accolades for the cavalry's success on the officers and men of Merritt's division. He could not offer enough adulatory comments about the "the boys," Merritt and Custer and their efforts in the battle.[7]

---

[6] Thomas T. Munford, "Reminiscences of Cavalry Operations," *Southern Historical Society Papers* 12 (1883): 450.

[7] *O.R.*, ser. I, vol. 43, pt. I, 498.

Further claims came thirty-four years later from Colonel James Schoonmaker of the 14th Pennsylvania Cavalry, by then a Gilded Age millionaire. Schoonmaker relished his days as a cavalry officer. As the nineteenth century drew to a close, Schoonmaker turned his attention toward securing official recognition of his deeds of valor at the Third Battle of Winchester in the form of the Medal of Honor. During a visit to Washington, D.C. in 1898, Schoonmaker met with Secretary of War Russell A. Alger, himself of veteran of the 1864 Shenandoah Valley Campaign. Although they both served in Sheridan's army, their personal paths had not crossed during the war, as Alger was in a different division and left the army before the epic engagement at Winchester. During their meeting, Alger supposedly asked Schoonmaker if he had ever received a Medal of Honor for his cavalry charge at Winchester. He had not, but certainly coveted "that greatest of legacies I could leave my children." Alger took an interest in the case and requested that Schoonmaker write an account of his heroics at Winchester. Schoonmaker readily complied and the letter was forwarded to Alger by the Honorable John Dalzell, Schoonmaker's Representative in Congress. Dalzell endorsed the request, adding "Colonel Schoonmaker you know as a true and faithful soldier during the war. He is now one of the most influential and respected citizens of Pittsburg." Schoonmaker received his medal. Although it has come to be known popularly as an award for the capture of Star Fort, Schoonmaker himself described the moment he claimed for his glory as the capture of Fort Jackson on Fort Hill. The intervening years had clouded his memory somewhat, adding infantry and a battery of artillery to the fort's defenders and Schoonmaker's list of captures. It seems that Schoonmaker's memory consolidated the results of the entire charge from Rutherford's Farm to Winchester to include the captures of prisoners and artillery made before his command overran Fort Jackson as occurring at that location.[8]

Averell remained in command of his division through the battle of Fisher's Hill. There he followed his orders and

---

[8] J. M. Schoonmaker to Honorable Russell A. Alger, March 8, 1898, contained in Schoonmaker Medal of Honor file, National Archives and Records Administration, Washington, D.C.

when the battle was winding down, Crook requested Averell to assist with rounding up prisoners and protecting the infantry from guerrillas who were preying on stragglers, which he did. No orders came for him that night, but at daylight on the following day Averell's division continued the pursuit toward Woodstock. The "rough country" slowed his progress, but Crook affirmed Averell's action, telling Averell that he "had done exactly right" and to continue in his course unless other orders were received. No other orders arrived, but Sheridan reached Woodstock before Averell and was greeted in a surly manner. Sheridan complained that Averell "had made a mistake in not pursuing the enemy the night before," without asking what actions the New Yorker had taken or by learning any details of his situation. The two men debated the situation, but it was clear that Sheridan was dissatisfied with Averell and nothing he could say would change his commander's opinion. Averell then moved forward with his division and pursued the Confederates, capturing some prisoners, but found that Early's army had regained its order. Averell observed that the Confederate army "was fully on the alert and perfectly able to hold the position against five times my force." At 11:00 p.m., Sheridan relieved Averell of command and appointed Colonel William Powell, the senior brigade commander, to lead the division.[9]

Sheridan's relief of Averell after two major victories in which the New Yorker's command contributed to the successful outcome came as a shock to him. He already understood that he was an outsider in the Cavalry Corps that was dominated by the Army of the Potomac elements and felt that his contributions were not acknowledged or worse. "Whenever I had an opportunity, my successes were barely mentioned, my activity was covertly censured, and an unjust impression was permitted to rest in the mind of the General-in-Chief to the extent of causing him to send an optional order for my relief," Averell explained.[10]

Averell never forgave Sheridan for relieving him of command in the Valley. "An officer who has served the

---

[9] *O.R.*, ser. I, vol. 43, pt. I, 499-500.
[10] Ibid., 501.

Government nine years, who has suffered from wounds in battle, cannot without any assigned cause or pretext be suddenly relieved from the command of a division whose record tells of nothing but success and victories without having his sensibilities outraged and his reputation jeopardized," Averell wrote. While Averell certainly thought highly of himself, ignored his failures, and exaggerated the importance of his accomplishments, he did not deserve the treatment that Sheridan had unleashed upon him. The incident effectively ruined Averell's military career.[11]

It would be five years before the paths of the two men crossed again. On that occasion, Sheridan greeted Averell as if they had last parted on good terms. Averell played along as a gentleman in the public setting, but afterward wrote Sheridan a scathing letter to set the record straight. "I was the victim of a grievous wrong or great mistake and I cannot permit you to entertain the impression from our exchange of civilities this morning that I am willing to resume friendly intercourse with you until some explanation from you of our actions on the occasion I have referred to has been received by me." Sheridan did not reply, but Averell had the last word.[12]

---

[11] *O.R.,* ser. I, vol. 43, pt. I, 500.
[12] Eric J. Wittenberg, *Little Phil: A Reassessment of the Civil War Leadership of Gen. Philip H. Sheridan* (Dulles, VA: Brassey's Inc., 2002), 114.

"To Aid the Union Cause"

The African American Experience in Clarke, Frederick, and Warren Counties as Revealed through the Records of the Southern Claims Commission

Jonathan A. Noyalas

Established on March 3, 1871, the Southern Claims Commission aimed to reimburse "loyal adherents to the cause and Government of the United States during the war, for stores or supplies taken or furnished during the rebellion for the use of the army of the United States in States proclaimed as in insurrection."[1] While the Southern Claims Commission records offer tremendous insight into the conflict's impact on the landscape and civilians, the testimony accumulated during the investigation for each claim reveals much about loyalty, efforts of civilians to assist Union soldiers throughout the conflict, and the contributions of Unionists to the Union war effort. Additionally, the testimony provided by the claimant and witnesses offers considerable understanding into the personal experiences of African Americans during the conflict, both those enslaved and free.[2]

In the lower Shenandoah Valley counties of Frederick,

---

[1] "The Southern Claims Commission," *The American Law Times* 4 (March 1871): 51.

[2] For further discussion about the operations of the Southern Claims Commission see Frank W. Klingberg, *The Southern Claims Commission* (Berkeley, CA: Octagon Books, 1978); Susan Michelle Lee, "Contested Unionism: William Pattie and the Southern Claims Commission" in *Virginia's Civil War*, ed., Peter Wallenstein and Bertram Wyatt-Brown (Charlottesville: University of Virginia Press, 2005), 201- 215; For discussions of the Southern Claims Commission in the Shenandoah Valley see Edward L. Ayers, *The Thin Light of Freedom: The Civil War Emancipation in the Heart of America* (New York: Norton, 2017), 469-474.

Warren, and Clarke, 149 individuals filed claims. Of the ninety-six who submitted a claim in Frederick, only twenty-five received compensation. Officials awarded money to ten of the twenty-seven claims filed in Warren County. Only nine of the twenty-six claims filed by residents of Clarke County were reimbursed. Among the total number of claims from individuals in these three counties, five were submitted by African Americans, one of which—a claim submitted for $200 by Meshack Johnson of Frederick County—was disallowed. The four claims that received a financial award from the Southern Claims Commission, excerpted below, reveal the war's toll on a segment of the lower Shenandoah Valley's enslaved and free black population during the Civil War and highlight their perspectives on freedom, the conflict, and support for the Union war effort.[3]

Claim of Washington Wells, Warren County[4]

Born free about 1816, Washington Wells labored as a farmer on a sixteen acre parcel of land he rented from Joshua McKay in Cedarville, Warren County.[5] At the time of the 1860 census Wells owned personal real estate valued at $455.[6] Wells filed a claim for $462 in 1876 for the loss of one mare, 200 bushels of corn, two tons of hay, four sheep, and seven hogs. The Southern Claims Commission awarded Wells $257.[7] The excerpts from Wells' claim which follow include the summary of the investigation, testimony from members of the McKay family, and Alfred Ashby, a free black man from Warren County.

---

[3] Data derived from Frederick County, Virginia, Southern Claims Commission, Claims Allowed, National Archives & Records Administration, Washington, D.C. (hereafter cited as SCC); Clarke County, Virginia, SCC; Warren County, Virginia, SCC; Frederick County Virginia, Southern Claims Commission, Claims Barred and Disallowed, National Archives & Records Administration, Washington, D.C. (hereafter cited as SCCB&D); Clarke County Virginia, SCCB&D; Warren County, Virginia, SCCB&D.
[4] Claim No. 11082, Washington Wells, SCC.
[5] Ibid.
[6] 1860 U.S. Census, Warren County, Virginia, August 26, 2020, Ancestry.com.
[7] Claim No. 11082, Washington Wells, SCC.

PETITION.

To the Honorable Commissioners of Claims,

Under the Act of Congress of March 3, 1871, Washington, D. C.:

The Petition of *Washington Wells*

respectfully represents:

That he *is a* citizen of the United States and resides at present *Ninorts Warren County, Virginia*

That he has a claim against the United States for *1 Mare, 200 Bush. Corn, 2 Tons Hay & 4 Sheep taken by order of Genl. Banks in May 1862, and used by the U. S. Army*

as follows:

1862

1 Mare, worth at least	150	00
200 Bushels Corn, at $1 per bush.	200	00
2 Tons Hay, at $15 per ton	30	00
4 Sheep, at $3 each	12	00
7 Hogs, at $10	70	00

Total value of Property, *taken* $462 | 00

Claim of Washington Wells seeking $462 in reimbursement.
(*National Archives and Records Administration*)

Summary of Claim

Claimant was a free born colored man who lived in Warren Co. Va. In 1862-3-4 he worked on shared land that belonged to the estate of Joshua A. McKay deceased who died in 1861.[8] The claim is for property taken in 1862. Prices at the time had not appreciated beyond the prices before the war. There was taken from him for the use of the army a mare, a quantity of corn, two tons of hay, four sheep, and seven hogs. The hay & sheep are charged at a fair value. The mare, hogs & corn are charged at about double their value at that time. There is testimony to show that 200 bushels of corn were taken but it is not certain that amount was taken. No voucher or receipts were given. We recommend the payment of $257.

That all the items in the above schedule were of the full value therein set forth and were taken from your petitioners for the use of and were used by the United States army under the following circumstances to wit: 1 mare taken by Col. Boyd's Regiment of Pa. Cav[al]ry. Vols. on or about the 12th day of May, 1864.[9] 200 bushels corn taken by General Wilson's Cavalry on or about the 1st day of October 1864; 2 tons hay taken at the same time, and the 4 sheep were taken by the Sixth Corps, under command of General [Horatio G.] Wright & the 7 hogs were taken at the same time on or about the 30th day of September 1864.[10]

---

[8] Joshua Antrim McKay was born on January 7, 1811, and died on July 16, 1861. He is buried in the Nineveh Presbyterian Cemetery in Warren County. Joshua Antrim McKay, U.S., Find A Grave Index, 1600's-current, August 28, 2020, Ancestry.com. At the time of the 1860 census McKay enslaved two individuals, a forty-three-year-old female and a fourteen-year-old male. Additionally, records indicate that at the time of the 1860 census McKay rented two enslaved males, one aged fourteen and another aged twenty-three. 1860 U.S. Census-Slave Schedule, Joshua A. McKay, August 28, 2020, Ancestry.com.

[9] Colonel William H. Boyd, 21st Pennsylvania Cavalry. For additional information about some of Boyd's exploits in the Shenandoah Valley see C. Armour Newcomer, *Cole's Cavalry or Three Years in the Saddle in the Shenandoah Valley* (Baltimore, MD: Cushing & Co., 1895), 82-88.

[10] Although a reference to General James Wilson, the Union cavalry division that Wilson commanded at the outset of Sheridan's 1864 Shenandoah Campaign was commanded by General George Armstrong Custer by October 1864. Jack H. Lepa, *The Shenandoah Valley Campaign of 1864* (Jefferson, NC: McFarland, 2003), 171-172.

Deposition by Members of the McKay family

The Rebels took corn and bed clothes from him in the 2nd year of the war; they fed the corn to their horses—never has received any pay therefore. [Washington Wells] was threatened by a Rebel officer who said he would shoot him if he did not tell where some Yankees were hid; said Rebel Officer put the pistol to his head; don't know whether it was cocked or not, was scared too badly... [Wells]Has given many a meal to United States soldiers, cooked for Genl. [William] Powell... [Wells] has always been in favor of the United States Government from the beginning of the war until the close of it.[II] Has talked with the Union soldiers... but was afraid to say anything to the generals. His sympathies always [rested] with the cause of the United States—never did anything against the cause.... Was never a slave, was born free... When his mare was taken, there was a Captain near & who belonged to Col. Boyd's Regt, he followed his mare to Camp & begged the Captain to let him have his, but that Captain told him he could not, for he must have a horse for his was broken down. When the hay was taken by the troops of Genl. [Horatio G.] Wright, an officer was present... as to the corn an officer came with wagons and horses took the corn out of the field; he shows there was an officer with them because the soldiers called him Captain & he belonged to Genl. Wright's command... The officers said they must have the corn, wanted it for the horses; claimant begged to have it for his boys, but the officer said they must have it for the horses, it was a troop of cavalry who took it. Don't know what regiment he belonged to. The same party took the sheep & the hogs; he does not know whether the officers commanded them both or not. They killed the sheep and the hogs & then put them on their horses and went off with them, the officer wasn't there when they went off. They were all together... he [Wells] know they took them to camp because he asked them when they were taking them off what he, claimant, would do for something to eat & they told him to come to camp and they would give him something to eat. That he went, that they gave him some food. Claimant asked for no voucher. All the property was taken in the day time... Guard Hill was 2 or 3 miles from where claimant lived, Genl.

[II] William H. Powell, who by the end of the 1864 Shenandoah Campaign commanded the second division of Sheridan's cavalry, was promoted to brigadier general on October 19, 1864. For further discussion see Ezra J. Warner, *Generals in Blue: Lives of the Union Commanders* (Baton Rouge: Louisiana State University Press, 1992), 384-385.

Wright camped there for a week or two, no battle or skirmishes occurred at that time that claimant knows of.

Deposition of Alfred Ashby[12]

Alfred Ashby, colored witness for claimant, who being duly sworn deposed and says that he is 38 years old, is a farmer by occupation, lives near Nineveh within the county of Warren & has been living there since March 1862, lived about half mile from claimant, saw Wells frequently during the interval from March 1862 to April 1865, sometimes everyday, sometimes at intervals of a few days. Had frequent conversations with claimant about the war; both hoped that the United States Government would succeed, they often expressed that hope to each other, both had made arrangement to leave the county with United States troops, but were delayed from time to time, but the difficulties which their having families to take along and provide for presented—never had any of the conversations in the presence of others except when those others were colored people, they dared not do it. Had often heard the "Secesh" talking about the people generally and the claimant Washington Wells, by name, as a "Union fellow." The Union people, white & blacks, regarded the claimant as a loyal man; don't know that the claimant ever gave information to the other side. Has heard "the Secesh" make threats of what they would do with claimant for Union sympathies; they said "he (the claimant) ought to be clubbed and hung." Claimant never contributed anything to the Confed[erate] Govt or army that witness knows of. Has never heard claimant's loyalty questioned. Witness is satisfied that claimant could not have established his loyalty to the Confederacy, because of his conversations with witness, in which he constantly expressed hope that the United States Government would succeed in overthrowing the rebellion; because claimant told a colored man, in the presence of the witness, to go tell John Garner, who had left the rebel army and who was trying to get out of the county and go north, that the rebel bushwhackers were about hunting up all those who had thus escaped.[13]

---

[12] At the time of the 1860 census, Alfred Ashby was a free black day laborer. 1860 U.S. Census, Warren County, Virginia, August 26, 2020, Ancestry.com.

[13] An examination of Confederate Compiled Service Records reveals 112 individuals with the name John Garner—none of those records indicate that anyone with that name deserted from the Confederate service.

Claim of Savery Iverson, Clarke County[14]

Born about 1801, Savery Iverson was enslaved at Carter Hall in Clarke County at the Civil War's outset.[15] In 1875 Iverson filed a claim for $161—the amount he deemed suitable reimbursement for the loss of his horse, saddle, bridle, and halter. The Southern Claims Commission awarded Iverson $100. In addition to the summary of the claim, the excerpt below also includes Iverson's testimony about the loss of his horse in 1864.

Summary of Claim

The claimant a colored man lived near Winchester Va. He did what he could to aid the Union cause—attended the sick, gave information to Union soldiers. He had a horse. In the fall of '63 a party of four (one an officer) took his horse and went to their camp at Winchester with him & told him he should have his pay. He objected. The taking is shown by himself & a colored woman—others were present but he says he is too poor to pay the expense of taking their testimony. We think the evidence sufficient & allow for all $100.

Statement of Savery Iverson

I have lived all my life at Carter Hall near Millwood... I was farming during the war. I have never been farther than Winchester. I went there to see about my daughter never took any oath or affirmation to the Confederacy of any kind... I have contributed to the Union cause and taken them to barns to stay at night and attended them when sick and have answered questions and given them what information I could... I wanted the Union cause to succeed all the time, said so to my friends. I always did all I could for the Union cause.... I saw all the articles claimed taken... It was about the middle of the war. I do not know the year, think it was in September all the property was at Carter Hall at the time it was taken. They were taken by U.S. troops an officer was present...I went with

---

[14] Claim No. 4983, Savery Iverson, SCC.
[15] 1870 U.S. Census, Clarke County, Virginia, August 26, 2020, Ancestry.com; Thomas D. Gold, *History of Clarke County, Virginia* (Berryville, VA: Thos. D. Gold, 1914), 42-43.

them in the field to assist in catching Mr. Burwell['s] horses.[16] Could not catch Mr. Burwell's horses & they took mine. I don't know the name or rank of the officer, they said they have ridden their own horses down & must have fresh ones they took the horse saddle, bridle & halter to Millwood where the troops were. I protested against them taken my horse and wanted them to take Mr. Burwell's as I had but one they said they could not help it, but would pay me for it. The property was taken down to Millwood where the other troops were. I followed the property about an hour after to Millwood, did not see it—saw the colonel don't know his name, complained to him about the taken of the property—he said old man just hold on you shall have pay for your property. I never got any pay or receipt. I saw them lead the horse away... I did not know any of the quarter masters or officers of the army. He was a grey horse of good size

Claim of Taylor Thornton, Clarke County[17]

Born about 1810, Taylor Thornton was enslaved at the Civil War's outset by the McCormick family. In 1877, Thornton sought compensation for $30.50 for flour and pork taken in 1864 by troops from Union general Philip H. Sheridan's Army of the Shenandoah. Thornton received the full amount of his claim. Fifteen years after the Civil War's end Thornton resided in Long Marsh, Clarke County, with his wife, Ellen.[18] In addition to the brief summary of Thornton's claim the following excerpt includes Thornton's statement.

Summary of Claim

Claimant is a colored man. His loyalty is established... the property for which compensation is asked was taken by a part of Sheridan's command in the day time.

Statement of Taylor Thornton

---

[16] A reference to George Burwell, the owner of Carter Hall. For a brief discussion of Burwell (1799-1872) and Carter Hall see Mary Gray Farland and Beverly Byrd Greenhalgh, *In the Shadow of the Blue Ridge: Clarke County, 1732-1952* (Richmond, VA: William Byrd Press, 1978), 44-45.

[17] Claim No. 55264, Taylor Thornton, SCC.

[18] 1880 Census, Clarke County, Virginia, August 26, 2020, Ancestry.com.

My name is Taylor Thornton. My age is 68 years I was born in the county of Clarke which was then a part of Frederick County. I have resided in Clarke County since it was made a county. My occupation is a day labourer. I have been engaged as a labourer all my life since I was able to work. I was a slave... and lived in Clarke County near the Shenandoah River & from the beginning of the war I worked about in the neighborhood and made my home at George [Carter] Blackmore where my wife lived. He owned my wife. She was the slave of Mr. Blakemore.[19]

Claim of Milford Jones, Frederick County[20]

Milford Jones, a free black man who lived in Frederick County, north of Winchester at the Civil War's outset, was born about 1820.[21] In 1876 Jones submitted a claim for $132.14 to reimburse him for the loss of wood, bacon, lumber, and pork. Jones not only lost those items, but lost his entire log home in the winter of 1864-65 when Union soldiers razed the structure and repurposed the logs for the construction of winter huts which comprised Camp Sheridan, north of Winchester near Stephenson's Depot. In addition to the summary of the claim and Jones' testimony, the excerpt below includes a statement from George Castleman.

Summary of Claim

The client is a colored man—was born free & is proven loyal by his own evidence and that of his neighbor Castleman. The army tore down his log house 40 x 17 & carried it to camp to help build their huts in the winter of 64-5. They took it all away on a train of 5 wagons. Rails also taken for fuel.[22] Corn taken day before—a hog stolen by one soldier.

---

[19] Born in 1815, George Carter Blakemore enslaved eleven people at the time of the 1860 census. Three of those whom he enslaved were female. More than likely the individual Thornton refers to as his wife was listed in the 1860 slave schedule as a fifty-five-year-old female enslaved by Blakemore. 1860 Census, Clarke County, Virginia, August 30, 2020, Ancestry.com; 1860 U.S. Census-Slave Schedule, George C. Blakemore [Blackmore], August 30, 2020, Ancestry.com.

[20] Claim No. 41794, Milford Jones, SCC.

[21] 1870 Census, Frederick County, Virginia, August 26, 2020, Ancestry.com.

[22] For a discussion of life at Camp Sheridan and the toll the Army of the Shenandoah took on the supply of timber and building supplies see William

Testimony of Milford Jones

*From the 1st day of April 1861 until the winter of the last year of
the war I lived on my own land which contained 12 acres and is situated
in Frederick Co. Va all of it was under cultivations and had a good fence.
Sometime in the last winter of the war my house was pulled down by U.S.
soldiers. I then moved near Stephenson's Depot in this county. I was a day
laborer... While the Confederate army was encamped around my house I
had to get a pass to go to Stephenson's Depot to buy things out of the store
for my family... I was all the time a Union man. I do not know if I had any
influence... I was born free. I was never a slave. I bought the 12 acres of
land from Mrs. Brown. I made all the money that I have paid for it by
working on farms as a day laborer. I agreed to pay her $300 for it and I
have paid here all the money except $90... I was born in Frederick County,
Virginia. I have never gone into bankruptcy.*

Deposition of George Castleman[23]

*I have known the claimant for the last 20 years and lived within
one and a half miles of him during the war and ... I have [had]
conversations with him about the war, its course and progress and he
always said that he hoped the Union army would succeed. I do not know
if any one... I did not know him to be threatened or molested on account of
his Union sentiment nor did I know him to do any thing for the Union
army except for Genl. Averel[l] when the Rebels came.[24] I do not know
what year it was.. but his command [Averell's] was marching my Milford
Jones house at the time and Genl. Averel[l] asked the claimant where the
Rebels were and I heard him tell them that they were in Winchester. I did
not know him to own Confederate bonds or do any thing to aid... the*

B. Jordan, ed., *The Civil War Journals of John Mead Gould, 1861-1865* (Baltimore,
MD: Butternut and Blue, 1997), 444-447.

[23] Born about 1824, George W. Castleman, was a farmer who resided in
Frederick County, Virginia. 1870 U.S Census, Frederick County, Virginia,
August 30, 2020, Ancestry.com.

[24] General William Woods Averell. Although unclear at what point Jones
offered information to Averell he might have provided information in July
1864 prior to the Battle of Rutherford's Farm. For further discussion of this
action which occurred on July 20, 1864, see Scott C. Patchan, *Shenandoah
Summer: The 1864 Valley Campaign* (Lincoln: University of Nebraska Press,
2007), 127-151.

Book Reviews

Reexamining *Defend the Valley*

Defend the Valley: A Shenandoah Family in the Civil War by Margaretta Barton Colt. New York: Crown Publishers, 1994. ISBN: 0-518-59315-7.

Review by Jonathan M. Berkey

In December 1869 the Barton family, who had lived near Winchester for generations, joyously prepared for Randolph Barton's marriage to Agnes P. Kirkland. A few weeks before her nuptials, Kirkland received a letter from her future mother-in-law, Fanny, informing Agnes that she could not attend the ceremony. "My life for some years past has been a repetition of singularly severe affliction," she wrote. "While I fear it necessary to cultivate a serene and cheerful demeanour in the social circle, I am aware of a shattered nervous system that would be unable to maintain even the appearance of calmness in a festive scene." (388) In the decade before she wrote to Kirkland, Fanny lost her husband, a brother, six of her ten children, and two sons-in-law. In *Defend the Valley*, Margaretta Barton Colt, Randolph's great-granddaughter, chronicles the tragic losses along with the excitement, challenges, and dangers faced by this Shenandoah Valley family on the home front and battlefield during the Civil War years. Colt consults a rich array of sources to tell her tale. Nine of the ten children of Fanny and David W. Barton left behind source material, as did both parents, Fanny's stepmother, three aunts and uncles, a brother-in-law, three grandchildren, a few cousins, and two slaves.

Six Barton brothers, a brother-in-law, an uncle, and several cousins saw active service in the war. Marshall Barton was killed at the First Battle of Winchester near his home; David Barton met his death at the battle of Fredericksburg. Strother Barton suffered a leg wound at the battle of Mine Run in November 1863 that required amputation. This wound weakened his stamina and likely shortened his life; he died in 1868 at age twenty-nine. The three Barton brothers who survived the war decade had varying experiences. Following a few attempts to adapt to the rigors of army life, Robert Barton left military service permanently after enduring the rigors of the 1862 Valley campaign. Bolling served as a cadet at the Virginia Military Institute and saw action at the battle of New Market. Randolph soldiered on through Appomattox, suffering five major wounds.

The Barton correspondence reveals a strong sense of kinship, humor, and liveliness among family members. Readers can feel the pressure faced by Bolling Barton as several well-meaning relatives ask about his spiritual state, some noting that he was the only family member who had not yet embraced Christianity. They might chuckle at the brotherly antics of Robert Barton, who intercepted one of Randolph's letters to Bolling and took the enclosed $20. To his credit, Robert did add a brief note to the letter admitting his crime before sending it on its way.

Other family details tug at the heartstrings. When setting up housekeeping in later years, Fanny would inquire about the dark stains on a beloved carpet. Family members kept the secret that they were the bloodstains of her son Marshall, whose body had lain in the family parlor after the First Battle of Winchester. Strother Barton wrote to his brother Robby of an incident when he got up in the night forgetting that his leg had been amputated and tried to walk on it, causing a painful fall. Small details like these highlight the human side of family experiences amid wartime suffering.

Accounts of the Bartons' slaves add layers of complexity to the family history. At times the Bartons and their slaves seem to have enjoyed friendly relationships. White family members reported the gratitude of slaves upon receiving financial gifts; they reciprocated by passing along kind words or food to their white benefactors. In one remarkable letter, the slave Sukey asserted that her master and mistress were more than just masters to her and that she was never a Yankee. A few months after writing this letter, Sukey fled to the Union lines. A similar ambivalence appears in a postwar letter from former slave Flora Braxton Turner to Robert Barton. Turner expressed thankfulness for a financial gift from Barton, and then asserted that the money reminded her of when she used to take care of Barton when he was a child. This curious passage at least hints that what Barton considered a gift, Turner interpreted as compensation for labor performed long ago.

The coverage of the Bartons' slaves illustrates some of the limitations of Colt's work. A few sections of *Defend the Valley* would benefit from more editorial analysis. Colt tends to take white family members' views of their slaves at face value. Some sections of the book rely entirely on postwar memoirs, which can be especially problematic when used as sources for prewar and wartime views of slavery.

These limitations aside, *Defend the Valley* provides a compelling and complete look at one family's experience throughout the Civil War era and adds to the rich mosaic of primary sources on the conflict in the Shenandoah Valley.

Jonathan M. Berkey is professor of history at Concord University in Athens, West Virginia, and the author of various essays and chapters about the Civil War era in the Shenandoah Valley.

The Great Partnership: Robert E. Lee, Stonewall Jackson, and the Fate of the Confederacy by Christian B. Keller. New York: Pegasus Books, 2019. ISBN: 978-1-64313-134-4.

Review by Jennifer Murray

To be sure, there are no shortages of scholarly or popular studies on Robert E. Lee or Thomas "Stonewall" Jackson, two of the Civil War's most famed generals. Christian Keller's *The Great Partnership: Robert E. Lee, Stonewall Jackson, and the Fate of the Confederacy* offers more than another biography on these two iconic generals, but as the title suggests, a study of the partnership forged between Lee and Jackson between 1862 and 1863. Indeed, Keller is ideally situated to take on such a topic. A professor of history at the United States Army War College, an institution devoted to graduate-level instruction for the nation's senior military leaders, Keller is expertly prepared to explore and analyze the Confederacy's senior leaders.

The Lee-Jackson relationship was built on, and flourished under, mutual trust, friendship, and shared religious faith. Keller's narrative starts in mid-June 1862 and traces the establishment and growth of this command relationship, and indeed friendship, through Jackson's death at Chancellorsville in May 1863. While

Jackson did not record a distinguished performance in the Seven Days Campaign, the two generals had developed a powerful personal and professional bond in the ensuing months. This relationship provided tangible results, bringing the Army of Northern Virginia a string of successful campaigns. Indeed, as Keller makes clear, the Lee-Jackson relationship was symbiotic. Moving beyond the discussions of Jackson as a brilliant tactician, Keller makes clear that Jackson was a skilled strategic-level thinker. Jackson had supported an invasion of the North in 1861, and although rebuffed by Richmond officials at that time, as he found himself a principal confidant to Lee, Jackson continued to advocate for taking the war to the North. Lee relied on Jackson and quickly the taciturn general became Lee's most trusted confidant.

Stonewall Jackson's death was a "strategic level inflection point," a "war-changing event." (176) Keller devotes a chapter to the reaction to the news of Stonewall's death. This is a tricky topic because it forces the writer to disentangle the historical event from generations of Lost Cause ideology and propaganda. Keller explores the reactions in the Army of Northern Virginia and the southern home front to survey how civilians processed and understood the news of Jackson's death.

Keller leaves no doubt that the relationship between Lee and Jackson was irreplaceable. "It was an imperfect team" he argues, "but it was superior to anything its opposite in the Army of the Potomac had yet produced." (206) In the final chapter, he tackles the implications of Jackson's absence in the Gettysburg Campaign. "What if Stonewall Jackson had been at Gettysburg?" is an enduring, entertaining hypothetical question for Civil War and Gettysburg enthusiasts and scholars alike. More than an exercise in hypotheticals, Keller provides a substantive exploration of *how* Jackson's death influenced the Gettysburg Campaign. Undeniably Jackson's death was a turning point in the command structure of the Army of Northern Virginia, and as Keller argues, the Army of Northern Virginia in the Gettysburg Campaign "suffered serious lapses in strategic unity of purpose, operational and tactical command and control, and seasoned judgment at all three levels of war." (214) Certainly, both A.P. Hill and Richard Ewell proved mediocre corps commanders. Keller addresses whether or not James Longstreet fully embraced the strategic purpose in a northern invasion, an unresolved question because of the discrepancies in Longstreet's wartime and postwar writings.

In a climate where writing about military history, much less Confederate history, has fallen out of vogue with academics, this is a gutsy book. Masterfully written with vivid prose, Keller produces a thoughtful analysis of a relationship at its highest levels, and, highest stakes. Readers interested in exploring how Lee and Jackson thought about war and strategy, or how they forged a command relationship, will find much of value in this book. When prophesizing the consequences of Jackson's death, Lee confided to his brother, "who can fill his place I do not know." (238) Indeed, as Keller convincingly argues, some partnerships are simply irreplaceable. As there was no equivalent for a John Lennon and Paul McCartney relationship, there would be no substitute for the Lee and Jackson relationship, this one, of course, of much higher stakes.

Jennifer Murray is assistant professor of history at Oklahoma State University and the author of On a Great Battlefield: The Making, Management, and Memory of Gettysburg National Military Park *(2014).*

The False Cause: Fraud, Fabrication, and White Supremacy in Confederate Memory by Adam H. Domby. Charlottesville: University of Virginia Press, 2020. ISBN: 978-0-8139-4376-3.

Review by Kenneth W. Noe

Much of what you think you know about the Civil War is a lie. So warns historian Adam Domby in *The False Cause*, a new examination of the links between Confederate memory, politics, white supremacy, and old-fashioned greed in the Jim Crow South. It was Domby, then a University of North Carolina (UNC) student, who rediscovered veteran Julian Carr's horrific boast at the dedication of the campus "Silent Sam" soldier statue that he once "horse-whipped a Negro wench" in the streets of Chapel Hill. (20) That speech became a turning point in the campaign that eventually saw Silent Sam dragged down 105 years after its erection. With *The False Cause*, Domby aims to tear down much more of the edifice that Carr and his compatriots created.

Often returning to Carr and Chapel Hill, Domby focuses on

the Lost Cause in North Carolina. By the 1890s, many whites in the Tar Heel state were hypersensitive about North Carolina's gingerly embrace of the Confederacy. North Carolina voters never endorsed secession, the state led the Confederacy in the numbers of conscripts and deserters, and upwards of 15,000 men there donned Union blue. At the same time, the current decade brought its own turmoil. A biracial "Fusionist" alliance of Populists and Republicans briefly gained power until a vicious Democratic counterrevolution in 1898 mimicked the worst days of Reconstruction. In the aftermath, unapologetically white supremacist Democrats disenfranchised African Americans and established Jim Crow. They also erected close to fifty Confederate monuments across the state. Domby calls them "victory monuments," charging that they reflect the triumph of 1898 more than the men of 1861. (19) The "monument men" also endorsed a usable, if false, interpretation of the war years, that posited fictional white unity in the Confederacy, defended slavery while denying it was a major cause of the war, and told stories of faithful slaves while covering up racial atrocities. (29)

They also grossly distorted the history of the shooting war, often starting with themselves. "General Carr" had been a private, drafted out of the university in 1864 and detailed as a clerk in a regiment that never saw much action. Men such as Carr continually inflated the number of UNC men in uniform, exaggerated the state regiments' heroism on the battlefield until North Carolina became "farthest at Appomattox" and "last at Appomattox," and crafted glorious tales of courage completely out of whole cloth. At one juncture, Domby proves that the oft-published tale of Edward Cooper, a deserter who supposedly returned to the ranks after pleas from his noble wife, was a total fabrication.

Before long, lying about the war became an epidemic. Phony veterans attended soldier reunions and told whoppers about their exploits. When the state expanded its Confederate pensions after the 1898 coup, scores lied for money. Domby's sample estimates that up to 20 percent of pensioners dissembled about their service in gray, including deserters and former Union soldiers, leaving the surviving pension files untrustworthy for researchers. African Americans faked loyalty too. In 1927, the state established pensions for enslaved men who accompanied their enslavers to the army. Of the 121 North Carolinians who eventually received them, many fudged their ages, concocted stories of devotion, and pocketed the money as back pay for slavery if not as reparations. A few even made a living miming for appreciative whites.

In the end, as Domby observes, Carr and his co-conspirators were remarkably successful. Their fabricated view of the war survives today in courthouse monuments, highway markers, whitewashed books, textbooks, internet fantasies of "Black Confederate" soldiers, and other manifestations of popular culture. It also still undergirds white supremacy, as seen recently in the streets of Chapel Hill and Charlottesville. In his epilogue, Domby entreats historians to speak up and help Americans to stop lying about the Civil War. Grounded in previous Lost Cause studies, deeply researched, and written with real skill, *The False Cause* is a powerful call to arms.

Kenneth W. Noe is a native of Virginia and currently the Draughon Professor of Southern History at Auburn University. He is most recently the author of The Howling Storm: Weather, Climate, and the American Civil War.

Searching for Stonewall Jackson: A Quest for Legacy in a Divided America by Ben Cleary. New York: Twelve, 2019. ISBN: 978-1-4555-3580-4.

Review by Brian Matthew Jordan

The Richmond-based writer and Civil War aficionado Ben Cleary makes plain the objectives of his new book: "I wanted to understand what drew me to [Stonewall] Jackson, to the Civil War, and to the past; I wanted to understand Stonewall, his contradictions, secretiveness, and incredible fighting ability." (12) Cleary invites readers along on a quest that revisits Jackson's old haunts and ranges over his storied battlefields. His itinerary is a veritable Civil War bucket list: he stands atop Henry Hill; winds through the hills of West Virginia; tours the Kernstown battlefield with historian Gary Ecelbarger; tiptoes among Confederate tombstones in the Shenandoah Valley; pauses at countless wayside exhibits; experiences an Ed Bearss bus tour; contemplates the savagery of the Seven Days; follows in the footsteps of Jackson's Chancellorsville flank march; and even retraces the route of Jackson's funeral procession in Richmond. "Visiting and revisiting the sites," the author contends, "is absolutely essential to understanding what happened there." (12)

For better or worse, *Searching for Stonewall Jackson* invites comparison with the late writer Tony Horwitz's *Confederates in the Attic* (1998). Like Horwitz, Cleary is a clever prose stylist whose wry wit finds its way to the page. Yet unlike Horwitz, who offered readers a travelogue punctuated with telling historical asides, Cleary tends to interrupt extended historical narratives—mostly culled from secondary sources and familiar first-hand accounts—with often brief dispatches from his modern travels. These dispatches tend to fall flat, never fully engaging with the problem of Civil War memory or the politics of race in the twenty-first century. Horwitz produced a probing meditation on the place of the Civil War in Southern memory and culture; Cleary, writing in the wake of the sesquicentennial and amid calls for the removal of Confederate monuments, bristles at the "self-righteous rhetoric reinforcing the equation that the Confederacy equaled slavery and nothing more." (237-238) Unlike Horwitz, whose memorable characters supplied keen insight into the war's legacy, Cleary's encounters with fellow battlefield pilgrims are frequently missed opportunities; conversations either stall, stop short, or sidestep the war's substantive issues. The author, for example, meets a local homeowner who, after puzzling over the removal of a Confederate flag near the Savage's Station battlefield, fears "we're going to lose all our statues on Monument Avenue." Rather than probe the nature of her attachment to the Confederacy, Cleary joins in her lament; before long, their dialogue turns to the exploits of relic hunters. (187-188)

Cleary's battle narratives are mostly sound and engaging, but scholars will object to several of the book's precepts. For one, Cleary writes that "slavery was the cause of the war...but for most Confederates, protecting their homes and families was a far more powerful motivator." (5) Yet as the historians Stephanie McCurry, Chandra Manning, and others have demonstrated, many non-slaveholding whites and poor yeomen farmers believed that the peculiar institution was essential to the safety and security of their homes and families. Concepts of personal honor, domestic order, and white manhood were hopelessly entangled in the institution of slavery. Understandably, Cleary does not want to believe that men wielded muskets in defense of human bondage, but he neglects the extent to which Black slavery shaped notions of white liberty in the nineteenth century South. "Who would die for slavery?" the author asks agnostically. "Yes, it was the cause of the war, and absolutely indefensible, but there was so much more to the struggle and to the men themselves than that one fact." (238)

It's that "so much more," of course, that the author can never quite define; indeed, in the end, even Cleary acknowledges that his search for Stonewall Jackson has come up short. "I set out to understand him," Cleary remarks toward the end of the book. "I must confess that I do only slightly more than at the beginning" (331). Readers desiring a basic, fast-paced narrative of the war's eastern campaigns will be satisfied, but those yearning for a more substantive reflection on the meaning and legacy of Stonewall Jackson and his cause will need to look elsewhere.

Brian Matthew Jordan is chair of the history department at Sam Houston State University and author of Marching Home: Union Veterans and Their Unending Civil War, *a Pulitzer Prize finalist.*

American Citizen: The Civil War Writings of Captain George A. Brooks, 46th Pennsylvania Volunteer Infantry edited by Benjamin E. Myers. Mechanicsburg, PA: Sunbury Press, 2019. ISBN: 978-1-6200-61305.

Review by Eric Campbell

The people of the north are scarcely yet alive to the magnitude of this rebellion... they seem to have forgotten...that their fellow men are enduring untold hardships and dying upon the bloody battlefields of the south, whilst they sit in comfort and security at home... Come face the danger with us, put your shoulder to the wheel, spill some of your patriotic blood...and you will find the war will terminate much sooner... Move with us "on to Richmond,"... True, it will cost immense amounts of treasure and blood; many noble loves will be sacrificed, but the great principles of liberty must be perpetuated; our government...must be preserved. Let Pennsylvania then rally around the old standard, support our noble Governor in the pledges he has made in behalf of the State of which

*he is justly proud, respond promptly to his call, and before
the festive days of Christmas make the annual round you
will returned to your homes with the consciousness of
having performed a sacred duty, and earned the glorious
title of an "American Citizen." (297-298)*

Thus, Captain George Brooks, of the 46th Pennsylvania, wrote in support of President Lincoln's July 1862 Proclamation calling for 300,000 additional troops. Brooks' letters, both to his wife, Emily, and to his hometown newspaper, the *Pennsylvania Daily Telegraph*, along with his 1862 journal, have been published in *American Citizen, The Civil War Writings of Captain George A. Brooks, 46th Pennsylvania Volunteer Infantry*. Edited by Benjamin E. Myers, the book is 382 pages in length and is organized into fourteen chapters, which cover Brooks' entire military service in both the three-month 25th Pennsylvania Volunteers and his longer service as captain of Company D, 46th Pennsylvania. Somewhat unique for a Civil War correspondence collection are the first two chapters, which cover Brooks' pre-war life, including several letters before George and Emily married, when he was struggling to establish a printing business in order to win over his future father-in-law (who did not approve of Brooks, to the point of wishing Brooks would not return when he finally marched off to war in 1861).

Not all volumes of Civil War correspondence are worth the effort of publication. *American Citizen* is more than worthy, surpassing the standard of most such works. Not only was George Brooks an observant and articulate writer, but he encountered some of the more well-known personalities, and was involved in some of the most famous campaigns and engagements in the eastern theater (despite serving only 16 months). These include, but are not limited to, General Charles Stone, General Alpheus Williams, General Nathaniel Banks, General Samuel Crawford, Belle Boyd, General John Pope, General Thomas "Stonewall" Jackson's 1862 Valley Campaign (including the "Running Fight" on May 24th and the Battle of First Winchester on May 25th), the Battle of Cedar Mountain, the Battle of Antietam, and countless others.

Editor Myers has done a masterful job of researching and footnoting all the principal events and individuals mentioned in Brooks' writings, organizing his letters and journal entries in an extremely reader-friendly fashion, along with adding additional narrative to fill the gaps that existed in Brooks' correspondence. The book is wonderfully illustrated with excellent maps, both area maps, showing all of the movements by both the 25th and 45th Pennsylvania during Brooks' service, plus detailed battle action maps for First Winchester, Cedar Mountain, and Antietam.

The only criticisms that can be offered are relatively minor, but still somewhat irritating. Correspondence volumes such as this should publish all of a soldier's writings verbatim, in order to provide a complete record. However, when the battles of First Winchester and Cedar Mountain were covered, editor Myers switched his style to cover these events with detailed battle narrative of his own, using Brooks' writings as support. This decision meant that some of Brooks' writings (which are the main focus of the book) are lost, while the remainder of his correspondence covering these critical engagements plays a secondary role to the battle narrative. First Winchester already lacks enough primary sources, so to see some of Brooks' writings get cut is especially frustrating. This work also lacks an index and bibliography, a necessity in all good histories.

Overall, however, *American Citizen* is an excellent addition to the genre of Civil War soldier correspondence. It certainly adds a great deal to those seeking information on the perspective of soldiers who served in the Shenandoah Valley.

Eric Campbell has worked as a ranger-historian for the National Park Service for thirty-four years, at a variety of sites, including twenty-four years at Gettysburg National Military Park. He has been the chief of interpretation at Cedar Creek and Belle Grove National Historical Park, which interprets all of the Civil War sites in the Shenandoah Valley, since 2009.

The Loyal Republic: Traitors, Slaves, and the Remaking of Citizenship in Civil War America by Erik Mathisen. Chapel Hill: University of North Carolina Press, 2018. ISBN: 978-1-4696-3632-0.

Review by Kyle Rothemich

Erik Mathisen serves as research associate at Queen Mary University in London and provides an innovative perspective on citizenship and loyalty in *The Loyal Republic: Traitors, Slaves, and the Remaking of Citizenship in Civil War America*. Mathisen situated his study primarily in the Mississippi Valley before, during, and after the Civil War. Mathisen focuses on the concept of citizens' loyalty and how this concept defined the meaning of citizenship in both the Confederacy and the United States. This allows Mathisen to move beyond simply viewing loyalty as a political act, but rather as a "larger attempt to redefine citizenship and reckon with the power of nation-states, all at once." (2) Exploring the conflicting loyalties of southern slave owners, Confederate soldiers, southern statesman, and formerly enslaved African Americans illuminates how these groups solidified their definitions of loyalty following the Civil War.

Mathisen shapes his work chronologically by first exploring what citizenship meant to inhabitants during the Early Republic, which shows that loyalty to localities and states was more important than loyalty to the federal government. Citizenship had little to do with loyalty to the United States, rather it was an "accounting of who stood within the republic." (8) As the sectional crisis moved towards the election of Abraham Lincoln, notions of citizenship had little meaning.

Mathisen's second chapter explores the creation of the Mississippi state government as part of the Confederate States of America. Mathisen focuses his analysis on John Pettus, the first Mississippi governor. Pettus failed in creating a functional Mississippi state government due to the growth of the larger Confederate government and Federal troops' occupation of the Mississippi River Valley beginning in 1862. In Mathisen's view, Pettus' failed tenure demonstrates how the failure of state building created an environment where loyalty to a nation surpassed loyalty to a state.

The Confederate army also proved to be a space where the Confederate government attempted to teach meanings of citizenship to its soldiers. Mathisen examines public demonstrations in Confederate camps to highlight how loyalty was instilled into soldiers. Confederate deserters were publicly punished with whippings for their suspected disloyalty to the Confederate cause. Mathisen concludes his third chapter by foreshadowing the lasting impact that notions of Confederate citizenship would have on former Confederate soldiers after the Civil War and into Reconstruction.

The book's fourth chapter focuses on the history of emancipation with an emphasis on Andrew Johnson's administration and its relationship to loyalty. Mathisen looks at two groups broadly: newly freed African Americans and former Confederates. Government officials realized the future of a reformed United States was rooted in African Americans becoming part of the American citizenry. African Americans fled plantations and joined USCT units during the war in an effort to demonstrate their loyalty to the Union and promise for citizenship. However, following the war, Johnson collected "loyalty oaths" from former Confederate citizens as a way for them to rejoin the United States body politic. Mathisen's use of loyalty oaths as a source reaffirms Johnson's effort to reassert white citizenship and to deny meaningful citizenship to African Americans.

Mathisen's final chapter explores efforts by African Americans in the Mississippi Valley to secure their own land and property. Loyalty to the United States provided an avenue for formerly enslaved people to secure the lands of former Confederate "traitors." As the author points out, "the language of loyalty and rights to property of all sorts quickly became fused." (147) The federal government's promise to protect this property was often undermined by southern white lawmakers. This rise of local control and lack of continued support from the federal government led to rights of freedpeople being unprotected. Using documents from the Southern Claims Commission, Mathisen shows how African Americans attempted to show their loyalty to and support for the United States. The author concludes by wondering why tests of loyalty as a way to prove citizenship were never included in the Constitutional amendments passed following the Civil War.

Mathisen's examination of formerly enslaved persons' efforts to secure property provides a framework for historians studying Reconstruction in the Shenandoah Valley. Due to the Valley's proximity to the North, how did African Americans in the Valley attempt to "remake" their citizenship? Was this through acts of loyalty to the United States? Or through efforts to purchase and own land? Examining these questions will help historians draw more conclusions about the African American experience in the Shenandoah Valley following the Civil War.

Kyle Rothemich is a historian for the National Park Service at Cedar Creek and Belle

"So Much to Say": The Civil War Letters of Corporal Robert Bradbury, Battery D, First Pennsylvania Light Artillery edited by Jonathan A. Noyalas & Charles H. Givens. Winchester, VA: Shenandoah University's McCormick Civil War Institute, 2020. ISBN: 978-690822738.

Review by Kevin Pawlak

Civil War soldiers wrote millions of letters home between 1861 and 1865. Hundreds, if not thousands, of those collections have been transcribed and published while many more can be found and read in research repositories across the United States. So, will another series of transcribed letters further our understanding of the Civil War? In the case of *"So Much to Say,"* the answer is "yes."

Editor Jonathan Noyalas points out the worth of Robert Bradbury's letters and why they deserve to see the printing press. Bradbury revealed more than the standard soldier often did and wrote about more than simply food and weather (though those were important pieces of a soldier's life in the field).

He wrote home explaining his enlistment in the United States Army. "The country is now in great peril," said Bradbury in August 1862, "and can only be saved by the devotion of its brave citizens. Every person who is over eighteen and under forty-five years of age who by any possibility leaves his home, has only one manly course before him, he should shoulder his musket and go forth to aid the just cause in the fearful struggle" (19). Incredibly, despite his participation in one of the Army of the Potomac's worst defeats (the Chancellorsville Campaign), Bradbury's devotion to the Union remained steadfast throughout his service.

Unlike many other published volumes of letters, Bradbury and his Pennsylvania artillery comrades actively participated in just a handful of military campaigns, including the Chancellorsville Campaign and the 1864 Shenandoah Valley Campaign. Battle descriptions waiting to be quoted liberally by historians in their works are thus hard to come by in this slim volume. Regardless, this does not diminish the value of Bradbury's correspondence.

Robert Bradbury provided excellent depictions of life in camp, where Civil War soldiers spent a majority of their enlistment terms. Bradbury's letters portray a soldier's yearning for communication from home and the plague of boredom that affected soldiers in camp. His camp correspondence details his daily rations, the construction of quarters, and the improvisation of converting cracker boxes into mouse traps, among other amusing incidents.

The letters' narrative about camp life is valuable to documenting how soldiers passed their years of service to their country. Besides sharing his daily routine, Bradbury offers valuable insight into the mind of a politically astute Union soldier. Though he enlisted to save the United States, Bradbury adopted emancipation as a necessary war measure to crush the Confederacy and supported Lincoln's reelection in the fall of 1864.

Bradbury's letters exclusively cover his wartime service. Thankfully, the editors researched and documented Bradbury's postwar life which, due to the increased awareness of post-traumatic stress, is especially worthwhile to his story. He no doubt suffered physically from the hardships of campaign and life in camp. It cannot be proved, but the editors speculate the mental strain he suffered while in the army may have played a role in his gruesome death in 1909.

Bradbury's own words are excellently supplemented with footnotes that point readers to articles and books that explain Bradbury's actions and thoughts or expand upon what he wrote. These notes serve as a valuable guide to the major studies of Union soldiers and their experiences in the Civil War.

The fact that Bradbury's letters, now in the possession of the McCormick Civil War Institute, have seen the light of day over 150 years after they were written makes this volume a valuable contribution to the growing literature on the experience of the common soldier in camp, on the battlefield, and in the political sphere of the Federal army and the United States, at large.

Kevin Pawlak is a historic site manager for the Prince William County Historic Preservation Division and the author of three books about the Civil War.

Custer's Gray Rival: The Life of Confederate Major General Thomas Lafayette Rosser by Sheridan R. Barringer. Burlington, NC: Fox Run

Publishing: 2019. ISBN: 978-1-945602-08-5

Review by Brandon H. Beck

Confederate Major General Thomas Lafayette Rosser is little known to general readers outside of Virginia, maybe even to readers outside the Shenandoah Valley. This biography by Sheridan Barringer, *Custer's Gray Rival: The Life of Confederate Major General Thomas Lafayette Rosser*, should change that. Barringer relied heavily on Rosser's papers and letters from throughout his long life. He died in 1910. Rosser was born near Lynchburg, Virginia, in 1836, and he moved to Texas when he was thirteen years old. George Armstrong Custer, his roommate at West Point, called him Tex, but he spent almost all of his war years with the Army of Northern Virginia.

I don't think we will ever know much more about Rosser than what Barringer tells us. But to know Rosser is not necessarily to like him. He was a good cavalry officer, and, like Custer, absolutely without fear. The Army could have benefited from his presence at Gettysburg on July 3 and at Third Winchester; unfortunately, he was not at either of these battles. He was obsessed with ego, promotion, and rank, despite the fact that he rose in rank from lieutenant in the Washington Artillery of New Orleans to major general of cavalry. But he was ungrateful and even vindictive to those who did the most to further his career—especially J.E.B. Stuart. He perceived apparent slights as assaults upon his personal honor. He did, however, keep his animosities to himself and his wife.

His greatest rival, beyond himself, was his old friend Custer. Since Custer was about as unlikeable as Rosser, it is remarkable how much they liked each other and how much alike they were. Barringer writes, "In Rosser and Custer the frenzy of battle produced an almost mesmerizing state of mind, a rage and audacity..." He goes on to quote the very perceptive Colonel Theodore Lyman, General George Meade's ADC, "Most officers would go into any danger when it was their duty, but fighting for fun is rare...such men as Custer (and Rosser) attacked whenever they got the chance, of their own accord."

Rosser was a dangerous attacker and raider. His greatest days came in 1864, as at Craig's Meeting House in the Wilderness on

May 3, and especially under Wade Hampton at Trevilian Station on June 11–12. Both victories came largely at Custer's expense. Custer was extremely lucky not to have been captured, with his command, at Trevilian Station. But by the fall, the odds were too great against Rosser and Jubal Early in the Valley. Neither had any margin for error. On September 19, Sheridan defeated Early at Winchester. On October 9, in the midst of the Burning, Rosser made a huge error of judgment at Tom's Brook. Pursuing General Torbert's cavalry down the Valley, he moved too far and too fast toward Strasburg, outdistancing any support. Like Custer at the Little Bighorn in 1876, Rosser rode right through signs of danger and even warnings from his subordinates. He shrugged off Colonel Thomas Mumford's warning, snapping, "I'll drive them through Strasburg by 10 o'clock." Instead, he rode into a catastrophic defeat at the hands of Custer. Custer, in charge of a division in Torbert's command, outnumbered Rosser two to one, and won a smashing victory that became a rout, called the "Woodstock races" by the victors.

Rosser and Custer were personal rivals, but not blood rivals. Although it was not quite clear to me in Barringer's book exactly when this note from Custer to Rosser arrived, it is unique in the history of the War:

> *Tom,*
> *Do not expose yourself so. Yesterday I could have killed*
> *you.*

In the following spring, just days before the Surrender, Rosser saw himself in Major James W. Thomson, who was from Winchester and died at the Battle of High Bridge. Barringer gives a full citation of a eulogy delivered for Thomson in 1894 in the Stonewall Confederate Cemetery in Winchester. The speaker quoted Rosser:

> *Thomson and I rode out on the field together to watch the*
> *fight, for we were both wounded...Thomson rushed into*
> *the conflict with what seemed like a spirit of deathless*
> *devotion...into the ranks of the enemy...retreating into the*
> *woods, they continued to fight and it was in the midst of*
> *one of these squadrons that Major Thomson was last seen.*

Looking back from 1891, Rosser believed his greatest day came on April 9, 1865, at Appomattox Court House, where he led what he called the last Confederate cavalry charge of the war. He was not present at the surrender. He left the army to try to reach the trans-Mississippi, but he was captured.

Rosser and Custer had fought each other throughout the war. After the conflict they met for the last time, in 1873, in the Dakota Territory. Rosser was then leading a surveying team—the Yellowstone Expedition—for the Northern Pacific Railroad. Custer was second-in-command of the cavalry escort. They spent a warm and happy evening together in camp, recalling days stretching back to West Point. Custer rode out in the morning, and they never met again.

This fine biography is highly detailed, with good maps and illustrations, and is a good read for anyone interested in General Rosser or Confederate cavalry operations in the Lower Shenandoah Valley.

Brandon H. Beck, PhD is professor emeritus of history at Shenandoah University and the founding director of the University's McCormick Civil War Institute. He is the author of numerous books on Civil War history.

Michigan's Civil War Citizen-General: Alpheus S. Williams by Jack Dempsey. Charleston, SC: The History Press: 2019. ISBN: 978-4671-3864-2.

Review by Ryan Bixby

Having commanded troops at some of the most significant battles and campaigns of the American Civil War, including Antietam, Chancellorsville, Gettysburg, and the "March to the Sea," one must wonder how Brevet Major General Alpheus Starkey Williams has not received more attention from scholars. Excluding one biography, an edited collection of Williams's writings, and a doctoral dissertation, few works focus exclusively on Williams. Therefore, Jack Dempsey seeks to address this void in *Michigan's Civil War Citizen-General: Alpheus S. Williams*.

Before discussing Williams' Civil War record, Dempsey begins his book by briefly tracing Williams' years prior to the conflict, including his involvement in the Mexican-American War and with two local militia units in Detroit. With the outbreak of the Civil War, Williams parlayed his previous military experience into receiving the appointment of brigadier general with the First Brigade of Michigan Volunteers in 1861. Quickly becoming disappointed that he was only responsible for training soldiers, Williams sought in August 1861 an appointment with the United States Volunteers. Placed in command of the third brigade under Major-General Nathaniel Banks, Williams and his men fought against the famous Stonewall Brigade in the Shenandoah Valley. Dempsey notes that Williams became frustrated during the 1862 Shenandoah Valley Campaign as he felt that he and his men had not been provided with adequate support. Williams' feeling of being under-supported and overlooked remains a theme throughout the book as on several occasions Williams expressed his disappointment on being slighted for a promotion in rank.

Dempsey notes that despite not being promoted, Williams continued to admirably fulfill his duty as commander. Assuming the role of interim corps commander of the XII Corps of the Army of the Potomac during the Antietam campaign, Williams passed along a copy of General Robert E. Lee's Special Orders No. 191 to General George B. McClellan. Williams's leadership also proved essential after the death of Brigadier General Joseph K.F. Mansfield as Williams and his men held the right wing of the Union army near the North Woods. Despite Williams' demonstration of quality leadership at Antietam, he returned to commanding his division after the engagement. Williams displayed commendable foresight at Gettysburg by almost taking Benner's Hill on July 1, 1863. Dempsey argues that if Williams had proven to be successful in this attempt, the entire progression of the events surrounding Gettysburg might have changed. Despite not taking control of Benner's Hill, Williams helped the Union cause by fortifying Culp's Hill. Although Williams once again proved his military worth, Dempsey asserts that General George Meade failed to recognize Williams's role at Gettysburg and thus cost Williams another change at promotion. Transferred to the trans-Mississippi theater in the fall of 1863, Williams assumed command of the XX Corps of the Army of the Cumberland. Similar to his time with the XII Corps, Williams received temporary command of the XX Corps during the Savannah campaign, but eventually relinquished this command to Major General Joseph A. Mower. Only during the waning months of the war would Williams receive a promotion in rank to brevet major general, but by this point he had become disenchanted with the failure of Union leadership to recognize his dedication to the war effort.

Dempsey spends the last part of the book exploring Williams' postwar political service. Williams campaigned for the governorship of Michigan in 1866 but lost the election. After serving a three-year stint as American consular to the nation of Salvador, which today is the country of El Salvador, Williams ran for a seat in the House of Representatives. Serving in Congress for four years, Williams advocated for veterans' rights and civil service reform. Losing his second reelection bid in 1878, Williams died suddenly before having finished his final year in office.

In the last chapter of the book, Dempsey evaluates various regimental and personal writings that mentioned Williams during the Civil War. Reading more like a historiographical essay than the concluding chapter of a book, Dempsey analyzes how these different works discussed Williams in relation to his role in the Shenandoah Valley, Antietam, Chancellorsville, Gettysburg, and the Savannah campaign. Dempsey tended to select passages from these books that supported his assertion that Williams never received the recognition nor promotions that he truly deserved. Rather than reserving these references until the concluding chapter, the author might have been better served to have incorporated these passages into the main chapters of the book. Despite this observation, those looking to learn more about Brevet Major General Alpheus S. Williams should use Dempsey's work as a launching point for further studies.

Ryan C. Bixby is an instructor of history at Three Rivers College. Dr. Bixby has authored several book reviews which have appeared in such publications as the Journal of Southern History, Civil War Monitor, New York History, *and on H-NET. He also contributed to an edited collection,* Lesser Civil Wars: Civilians Defining War and the Memory of War *(2012).*

Notes on Contributors

Jake Gabriele graduated from Shenandoah University in 2018 with a BS in history and is currently enrolled in the PhD program in history at Mississippi State University. In the summer of 2018 Jake held the Dr. David and Mrs. Melanie Miles Summer McCormick Civil War Institute summer fellowship

Robert Grandchamp is the award-winning author of fifteen books on American military history, including *The Boys of Adams' Battery G, The Seventh Rhode Island Infantry, Rhody Redlegs*, and most recently *Rhode Island's Civil War Dead: A Complete Roster*. Robert earned his MA in American History from Rhode Island College. He is a former National Park Service Ranger with service at Harpers Ferry, Shenandoah, and Blackstone Valley. He is currently a senior analyst with the federal government and resides in Jericho Center, Vermont, with his wife Elizabeth, and their children.

Victor Herrera, an English and history major, graduated from Shenandoah University in 2020. During the summer of 2018 he held the Dr. David and Mrs. Melanie Miles Summer McCormick Civil War Institute summer fellowship.

Brandy N. Noyalas earned her B.S. in history from Shenandoah University in 2002. An award-winning educator, Noyalas teaches American History at Daniel Morgan Intermediate School, a post she has held for eighteen years. Additionally, she works as a volunteer with Shenandoah University's McCormick Civil War Institute at the Cool Spring Battlefield.

Jonathan A. Noyalas is director of Shenandoah University's McCormick Civil War Institute and founding editor of the *Journal of the Shenandoah Valley During the Civil War Era*. He is the author or editor of thirteen books on Civil War era history and has contributed more than 100 articles, essays, reviews, and book chapters to a variety of scholarly and popular publications including *Civil War History, Civil War Times, Civil War Monitor,* and *America's Civil War*. He is the recipient of numerous awards for his teaching, scholarship, and service including the highest honor that can be bestowed upon a professor at a college/university in the Old Dominion—the State Council for Higher Education in Virginia's Outstanding Faculty Award. His next book, *Slavery and Freedom in the Shenandoah Valley during the Civil War Era* will be released by the University Press of Florida in the spring of 2021.

Cheyenne Nimes holds MFAs from San Francisco State and Iowa and is an NEA fellow in poetry. Nimes' recent work has appeared in *Passages North* and *Ninth Letter* as well as in and the anthology *The Shell Game: Writers Play with Borrowed Forms* (University of Nebraska Press). Nimes is also the great-great-granddaughter of Ephraim Burket. She dedicates her contribution to this volume to Burket's memory and to all of the men from the 110th Pennsylvania Volunteer Infantry.

Kimberley Vanscoy Oliveto is a history major at Shenandoah University and was a contributing author to *"A Prominent Place": Winchester's 275 Years in 50 Artifacts*.

Scott C. Patchan is a graduate of James Madison University and is the author of many articles and books including *The Forgotten Fury: The Battle of Piedmont* (1996), *Shenandoah Summer: The 1864 Valley Campaign* (2007), *Second Manassas: Longstreet's Attack and the Struggle for Chinn Ridge* (2011), *The Battle of Piedmont and Hunters Raid on Staunton* (2011), and *The Last Battle of Winchester: Phil Sheridan, Jubal Early and the 1864 Shenandoah Campaign* (2013). He has also published articles in *Blue & Gray Magazine, Civil War Magazine, North & South, America's Civil War* and other historical publications. He is currently editing the journal of Colonel Joseph Thoburn and continuing his work on the Valley Campaigns.

Nicole Roland earned her bachelor degree in history from Shenandoah University in 2020. During the summer of 2020 Roland held the Dr. David and Mrs. Melanie Miles Summer McCormick Civil War Institute summer fellowship. She currently works as an interpretive historian at Fort Roberdeau near Altoona, Pennsylvania.

Shelby R. Shrader graduated from Shenandoah University in May 2017 with a BS in history. She was the first recipient of the Dr. David and Mrs. Melanie Miles Summer McCormick Civil War Institute summer fellowship. She reviews regularly for *Civil War News* and serves on the McCormick Civil War Institute's advisory board.

Steven R. Stabler is a history and political science major at Shenandoah University. He was a contributing author to *"A Prominent Place": Winchester's 275 Years in 50 Artifacts*.